Czech–Americans
in Transition

Edited by
Clinton Machann

EAKIN PRESS  Austin, Texas

FIRST EDITION

Published in the United States of America
By Eakin Press
A Division of Sunbelt Media, Inc.
P.O. Box 90159 / Austin, TX 78709
email: eakinpub@sig.net
www.eakinpress.com

2 3 4 5 6 7 8 9

1-57168-298-8

Library of Congress Cataloging-in-Publication Data

Czech-Americans in transition / editd by Clinton Machann.
    p. cm.
    "This collection of papers is based on presentations made at the 1997
Annual Meeting and Conference of the Czechoslovak Society of Arts and
Sciences . . . held July 12-13, 1997, at the Bell County Exposition Center in
Belton, Texas, in conjunction with . . . the 100th Anniversary of the Slavonic
Benevolent Order of the State of Texas"--Introd.
    Includes bibliographical references.
    ISBN 1-57168-298-8
    1. Czech Americans—Texas—Ethnic identity Congresses. 2. Czech
Americans —Texas—History Congresses. 3. Czech Americans—History
Congresses.
    I. Machann, Clinton.
    E184.B67C9   1999
    973'.049186--dc21   99-10925
                                                    CIP

Contents

iii

Preface

Remarks by the President of the SVU at the
Opening of the SVU Conference
"Czech-Americans in Transition:
Challenges and Opportunities for the Future"

Miloslav Rechcígl, Jr.

Your Excellency Ambassador Vondra, President Leshikar, Members of the Czechoslovak Society of Arts and Sciences, Distinguished Guests!

It gives me great pleasure to open this historical SVU [Czechoslovak Society of Arts and Science] Conference, during which a number of distinguished speakers will address some of the salient issues facing Czech-Americans today.

I am delighted to see so many non-members here. This gives me hope that some of you will soon join our ranks. Above all, I welcome among us the new Czech Ambassador Alexandr Vondra, who will stay and participate with us throughout most of the conference today. I am delighted to say that he is here, not only as a guest, but also as a recently joined member of our Society. Let that be an example for others!

I am pleased to have with us Mr. Howard Leshikar, President of the *Slovanská podporující jednota statu Texas* (SPJST—The Slavonic Benevolent Order of the State of Texas), who has graciously accepted co-sponsorship of our conference on the occasion of this historic milestone of his organization. I believe that the combination of the conference with the historical celebration of the 100th anniversary of the SPJST is a unique event which will mark the beginning of a "beautiful friendship" and future collaboration between the two organizations.

To be sure, we are not as old as the SPJST; nevertheless, since its inception in 1958, the SVU has grown into a respected international organization with chapters in major cities around the world. In a nutshell, the Society has organized eighteen world congresses, two of which were held in Prague and one in Brno. In addition the SVU has held six European and twenty American and Canadian conferences, and has sponsored more than thirty art exhibits, fifty musical and dramatic productions, and twenty book displays. It has published over eighty books and monographs and four periodicals, besides providing support for some fifty other publications.

We hope that this joint historic gathering of the SPJST and the SVU is only the first of many joint activities in the future. We have a lot in common, and we can benefit from each other. Our love for the country of our ancestors and the desire to preserve our cultural heritage abroad are our common denominators and could be the basis for future cooperation. The sons and daughters of SPJST members, as well as many SPJST members themselves, could clearly benefit from membership in our Society, with its linkages to major educational and cultural institutions throughout the world, including those in the Czech Republic and in Slovakia.

In closing, let me congratulate our Texan friends again on their important anniversary and express my sincere thanks to local organizers for all the preparatory work, particularly to Clinton Machann, who must be, by now, completely exhausted from my daily e-mail messages. I do hope that everybody will take advantage of the numerous activities that have been planned and that you will participate fully in various debates and meet all the interesting people, while having fun, as well.

Introduction

The SVU Conference in Belton

This collection of papers is based on presentations made at the 1997 Annual Meeting and Conference of the Czechoslovak Society of Arts and Sciences (*Společnost pro vědy a umění*, SVU), held July 12-13, 1997, at The Bell County Exposition Center in Belton, Texas, in conjunction with the celebration of an important historical event: the 100th Anniversary of the Slavonic Benevolent Order of the State of Texas (*Slovanská podporující jednota státu Texas*, SPJST).

Sometime in late 1996, SVU President Miloslav Rechcígl and I had a conversation about the feasibility of holding an annual meeting of the organization in Texas. Mila was aware of the fact that ethnic consciousness among Czech Americans in Texas was relatively high: not only were highly successful ethnic festivals held annually in West, Ennis, Caldwell, Praha, and several other Texas cities and towns associated with Czech culture, but recent projects such as the Texas Chair of Czech Studies at the University of Texas at Austin (funded by the Czech Educational Foundation of Texas), the Texas Czech Heritage and Cultural Center at La Grange, the Czech Cultural Center-Houston, and the expanded Czech exhibit at the Institute of Texan Cultures in San Antonio were unmistakable signs of a renaissance of Czech culture in the

State. Membership in the Czech Heritage Society of Texas and other Texas Czech clubs and organizations was higher than ever, while the more traditional fraternal organizations like the SPJST with a historically rural and small-town base were finding increasingly significant niches in metropolitan areas such as Houston and Dallas. And yet the SVU, with officers and a membership made up primarily of first-generation immigrants of the mid-to-late twentieth century and with an American membership concentrated in the Northeastern United States, had never met in Texas, where descendants of Moravian immigrants of the late nineteenth and early (pre-World War I) twentieth century formed the core of the Czech-American community.

Texas did, however, have a smattering of SVU members, of which I was one, and Mila Rechcígl and I agreed that the Centennial Celebration of the SPJST provided an ideal opportunity for SVU leaders from around the U.S. (and even outside the U.S.) and Texas Czechs to get better acquainted with each other and discuss their common goals for the preservation of Czech culture in the twenty-first century. In spite of its regional identity, the SPJST is one of the most successful Czech fraternals in the U.S., and Vice-President Leonard Mikeska's short historical account of that organization, which appears in this volume, suggests its vital importance to the Texas Czech community over the past hundred years. Members of the SPJST had good reason to celebrate their history and display their ethnic pride. From the beginning, President Howard Leshikar was enthusiastic about inviting the out-of-state guests from SVU to share in the celebration. President Leshikar and the SPJST proved to be most gracious hosts and cooperated in every way to make the SVU sessions a part of the general success of the magnificent week-end in Belton. Combining their resources, the two organizations were successful in securing the participation of Alexandr Vondra, the Ambassador of the Czech Republic to the United States, as well as several Czech officials from Prague. Of course, many state government officials and other prominent Texans were involved in the SPJST ceremonies.

The following letter (translated from the Czech by David Z. Chroust), sent to the conference by a Senator from the Czech Republic, speaks for itself:

Dear Friends,

I am taking advantage of the journey of my friend, chairman of the *Československý ústáv zahraniční* (Institute for Czechs Abroad), Mr. Jaromír Šlapota, to introduce myself to you. I am Vice-Chairman of the Committee on Foreign Affairs, Defense and Security in the Senate of the Czech Republic, and Chairman of the Senate's Committee on Czechs Living Abroad. In these two capacities I extend my greetings to you and wish you a successful conference. I greet all the Czech-Americans who are gathering to celebrate the one-hundredth anniversary of the *Slovanská podporující jednota statu Texas* (Slavonic Benevolent Society of the State of Texas).

Collaboration with Czechs, Moravians and Silesians living abroad is a completely new area of responsibility for me, but let me assure you that I have taken this responsibility very seriously and that I have begun to explore possibilities. The members of our Senate Committee want to take an organized, goal-oriented approach toward improving and deepening collaboration between the two communities, and we want to do this in ways that benefit both the homeland and our countrymen throughout the world. I want to assure you that our Senate committee will be receptive to all positive areas for improving ties between Czechs abroad and in the Czech Republic. I am convinced that we already have a considerable foundation upon which to build. As you know, the participation of Czech citizens abroad in elections in the Czech Republic is among the issues that are under serious consideration these days.

Our Senate Committee also can and would like to become a bridge between Czechs living in the West and those who settled in countries to the East. As you can see, we have much work ahead of us. Personally, I look forward to these tasks with pleasure, and I am counting on your support and collaboration.

Yours,
Senator Milan Špaček
Parliament of the Czech Republic
Office of the Senate

The SVU sessions themselves were only one small part of the centennial celebration, but there was an overwhelming response from scholars and Czech community leaders interested in contributing to our discussions on the following general topics:

"Ethnicity and the Preservation of Language and Culture;"
"Czech-American Centers, Archives and Libraries and Their Future;" and "Relations Between the United States and the Czech
Republic." In addition to SPJST President Leshikar and the authors
of the papers collected in this volume, speakers who took part in
five individual panels include the following:

Ronald Bartak, a director of the American Friends of the Czech
Republic who has served on the staff of the Central Intelligence
Agency, the State Department, and the House Armed Services
Committee; Dagmar Bradáčová, director of the Czechoslovak
Heritage Museum, Library, and Archives at the headquarters of
CSA Fraternal Life in Berwyn, Illinois; Retta Chandler, chairman
of the board of directors of the Texas Czech Heritage and Cultural
Center; Robert W. Doubek, president of the American Friends of
the Czech Republic; Michelle Fagan, librarian of special collections at the University of Nebraska at Lincoln; Bruce Garver, professor of history at the University of Nebraska-Omaha; Thomas G.
Gibian, a retired chemical engineer and former CEO of Henkel
Corporation who serves as a director of the Société de Chimie Industrielle, American Section, and two firms specializing in biomedical technology; Miroslav John Hanak, retired professor of
languages and comparative literature at Texas A&M University at
Commerce; Peggy Hanak, a retired teacher of psychology and special education; Milan Hauner, a historian who specializes in
Czech as well as South and Central Asian topics; George
Hlavinka, who has been instrumental in the development of the
Burleson County Heritage Museum in Caldwell, Texas; Zdeněk
Hruban, a retired professor of pathology from the University of
Chicago, where he established the Archives of the Czechs and
Slovaks Abroad; Vladimír M. Kabeš, an American specialist in international law who for many years held the position of Secretary-General of the International Touring Alliance in Geneva, Switzerland and has served as a foreign advisor to President Václav Havel;
Josef Kolínský, a director of the *Československý ústav zahraniční*
in Prague; Miroslav Koudelka, a Czech genealogist from Olomouc
whose books include *Czechoslovakia: A Short Chronicle of
27,094 Days* and an English translation of Jan Habenicht's *History*

of Czechs in America; Eugene Labay, legal advisor and chairman of the Board of Trustees of the Czech Heritage Society of Texas; Sylvia Laznovsky, president of the American Sokol Organization—Southern District; Carolyn Sumbera Meiners, secretary and publicity chair of the Texas Czech Heritage and Cultural Center; Larry Pflughaupt, a member of the Board of Directors of the Czech Cultural Center-Houston; Peter A. Rafaeli, who owns two auto dealerships and serves as a director of the American International Auto Dealers Association and Honorary Consul of the Czech Republic for the Commonwealth of Pennsylvania; Effie Rosene, chairman of the Board of Directors of the Czech Cultural Center-Houston; Clarice Marik Simpson, a member of the Board of Directors of the Czech Cultural Center-Houston; Daniela Sipkova-Mahoney, an Oregon artist, publisher of children's books, and business consultant who specializes in foreign language services; Robert L. Skrabanek, a retired professor of sociology from Texas A&M University who is the author of *We're Czechs* and several journal articles on the role of ethnicity in social change; Jaromír Šlápota, president of the *Československý ústav zahraniční* in Prague; Woody Smith, president of Texans of Czech Ancestry (TOCA) and the Russian language program coordinator in the Department of Modern Languages at Southwest Texas State University; Miroslav Synek, a poet and physicist who works as an independent consultant and researcher in the San Antonio area; Jaromír J. Ulbrecht, Foreign Member of the Academy of Engineering of the Czech Republic and a chemical engineer and technology consultant who has held positions in the Department of Commerce and worked with the Industrial Research Institute and various Fortune 500 Companies; Martha Wilding, librarian at the National Czech and Slovak Museum in Cedar Rapids, Iowa; and Ladislav Zezula, President of the Bexar County Chapter of the Czech Heritage Society of Texas and a member of the Czech Community Advisory Committee for the Institute of Texan Cultures in San Antonio.

I considered it an honor to serve as project director for the SVU program at Belton and work with these distinguished participants, as well as those whose papers and presentations are included in this volume. I also wish to acknowledge the assistance provided by Milton Cerny, Dagmar Hasalová White, and the other members and associates of the SVU, the SPJST, and several other Czech-American organizations.

Czech-American Cultural Centers, Libraries, and Museums

One highlight of the conference was a group of reports on cultural centers, libraries, and museums with a Czech theme, including several multi-media presentations organized by Texans of Czech Ancestry (TOCA). This group helps to coordinate, promote, and disseminate information about a wide range of Czech-related activities. In the planning stages are two particularly ambitious projects in Texas: the Texas Czech Heritage and Cultural Center in La Grange, and the Czech Cultural Center-Houston. The multi-functional facility in La Grange will seek to preserve and promote the history, language, culture, and heritage of Texans of Czech ethnicity who trace their ancestry to the Czechs who immigrated from the present-day Czech Republic, Czechoslovakia, or the former Austro-Hungarian Empire. The facility, to be located on the banks of the Colorado River, is being designed as a "Czech People's Center" with a library, archives, exhibit halls, auditorium, classrooms, meeting rooms, visitor information center, gift shop, and bookstore. The purpose of the Czech Cultural Center-Houston is to unify the Czech and Slovak community around issues of importance and provide a central focus for all things Czech-related, serving as a clearinghouse for useful information. The CCC organization aims to preserve, record, and celebrate the language, scholarship, and the arts of Bohemia, Moravia, Slovakia, and Silesia. It has already begun to sponsor musical and cultural events of special interest. A facility is being planned for the Museum District of Houston, one which will include a ballroom, meeting rooms, and a restaurant. As both the La Grange and Houston projects near completion in the coming years, Czech-Americans will indeed have cause for celebration.

A related presentation focused on the Czech Texan Exhibit at the Institute of Texan Cultures in San Antonio, which is being expanded to include features such as a touch-screen video system with narrated cinematic programs that include ethnic story-telling, music, language lessons, and the display of archive photographs. In addition, there were reports on the recently expanded Czech exhibits at the Burleson County Heritage museum in Caldwell and the Sokol Havlicek Borovsky Museum in Ennis, which was rebuilt and stocked with valuable new exhibits of artifacts and books after fire destroyed the building in 1990.

There were also reports on important collections of books, archives, and artifacts from around the United States that are of special interest to anyone conducting research in Czech and Czech-American history and culture: the Czechoslovak Heritage Museum, Library, and Archives at the headquarters of CSA Fraternal Life in Berwyn, Illinois; the major Czech collection that was built up by Joseph Svoboda at the library of the University of Nebraska at Lincoln; the important Archives of the Czechs and Slovaks Abroad built up by Zdeněk Hruban at the University of Chicago; and the National Czech and Slovak Museum at Cedar Rapids, Iowa—the largest and most complex facility of its kind—which helped to inspire the Houston and La Grange projects.

The formal and informal dialogues at the conference among so many individuals with different backgrounds, but similar interests, were bound to produce new ideas and initiatives. One tangible result of the Belton Conference was a proclamation entitled "The Preservation of Czech-American Cultural Heritage," jointly signed by SVU President Rechcígl and SPJST President Leshikar in the weeks following the conference. This initiative has already helped to inspire new efforts to identify and preserve historical sites and monuments. The momentum from the Belton conference carried over to a conference entitled "The Czech Republic and Czech Americans on Their Way to a Common Future," organized by Ambassador Vondra and held at the Czech Embassy in Washington, D.C. on October 18-19, 1997. Many of the participants at the Belton conference also took part in the Washington event, which included a presentation by U.S. Secretary of State Madeleine Albright. Officers and representatives of Czech-American organizations from around the United States met with Embassy officials and government officials from the Czech Republic, including Senator Michael Žantovský, to discuss strategies for broader cooperation. The conference participants approved a resolution with language similar to that of the Belton proclamation, calling for the establishment of the Cultural Heritage Commission, which will aid current organizations in gathering and disseminating information, thus coordinating and publicizing efforts to preserve the Czech heritage and develop Czech culture in America. Special interest was expressed in projects related to historical sites and monuments, the political influence of the Czech-American community, and the future economic and political cooperation between American and Czech business and political leaders.

Since then, officials from many Czech-American organizations have joined the SVU and SPJST in signing this document. In July of 1998, the Czech Ministry of Foreign Affairs awarded a grant to the SVU to help finance a survey of historical sites, monuments, and archival materials. This project will be coordinated closely with Czech institutions such as the Náprstek Museum in Prague, which holds the most extensive collections of Czech-American materials in the Czech Republic.

Organization of the Papers

The papers published in this volume are a sample of the over forty presentations made at the conference. In some cases, the papers are slightly edited versions of the actual speeches or lectures delivered at Belton. In others, the authors have taken the opportunity to revise and expand the original presentations. At the beginning is the text of Ambassador Vondra's address to the combined assembly of those attending the SPJST centennial celebration, and it contains a special message sent to Belton from President Václav Havel of the Czech Republic. The ambassador's commitment to meet and confer with Czech-Americans in order to strengthen cultural, economic, and political ties between Czechs and Americans is clearly illustrated by his presence at Belton and his organization of the October conference of Czech-American leaders soon afterwards. Although the political issue of NATO expansion (to include Hungary and Poland as well as the Czech Republic) was clearly a high priority at this time, Mr. Vondra has placed equal emphasis on cultural and economic matters.

Following the ambassador's remarks, the paper of Zdeněk Lyčka, director of cultural relations and Czechs Living Abroad within the Czech Ministry of Foreign Affairs, provides a historical context for the relations between Czechoslovakia (later the Czech Republic) and Czech emigrants and emigrant communities throughout the world. Then Leonard D. Mikeska, vice-president of the SPJST, gives a short history of the century-old host organization and lists sources for those who wish to learn more about this subject.

Next comes a cluster of essays which examine various aspects of Czech-American history and culture. SVU President Miloslav Rechcígl goes back to the origins of the Czech-American community in his overview of Bohemian and Moravian pioneers in colonial America. Peter Bísek, after taking a brief look at the historical development of the Czech-American press in America, reflects on its present state and looks toward its future with an optimism that may surprise some readers. Houston attorney Daniel Hrna offers personal comments on the significance of genealogy, and Leo Baca, known for his compilation of nineteenth- and early twentieth-century Czech immigration passenger lists for the ports of Galveston, New Orleans, and New York, gives practical advice to genealogists and family historians on documenting Czech immigrant arrivals. Three other essays have an especially regional focus: Joseph Roštinský discusses the function of Moravian folk songs in preserving Czech culture in Texas, Robert Janak surveys recent activities by the Czech Heritage Society of Texas that have strengthened ties between Texas Czechs and the Czech Republic, and, in a short historical account of the Czech Educational Foundation of Texas, I take a look at some of the regional leaders who helped strengthen the position of Czech language and culture in Texas by focusing on higher education.

The final three papers represent important current research topics of special interest to Czech-Americans. Milada Polišenská reports on new sources of information that illuminate the relationship between President T. G. Masaryk's Czechoslovakia and the U.S. government. Ludmila Dutková describes her ambitious ethnolingusitic study of Texas Czech, a project which incorporates a great deal of original fieldwork. David Zdeněk Chroust outlines the beginnings of his work on a biography of one of the most important and interesting Czech-Americans, Thomas Čapek (1861-1950), the attorney and banker who became the most prolific chronicler and interpreter of the Czech ethnic group in America. I believe that in all three of these studies we see previews of significant future publications.

A selected bibliography of English-language publications about Czech-Americans, compiled by Miloslav Rechcígl, appears at the end of this volume. It contains information about many recent publications and should be a convenient and useful reference tool for readers who want to know more about this subject.

As I write this introduction, the U.S. Senate recently has voted in favor of NATO expansion, another step towards a closer relationship between Americans and Czechs. Also, plans are being made for a series of high-profile conferences, exhibits, concerts, and other academic, political, and cultural events in Washington, D.C. in October 1998 that will commemorate the 80th Anniversary of the founding of Czechoslovakia. The recent political developments that began with the Velvet Revolution of November 1989 in Europe, combined with indications of a strong desire to preserve our ancestral heritage and historical memory in America, point toward a positive and potentially exciting future for Czech ethnicity in America.

A grant from the Texas A&M University Program to Enhance Scholarly and Creative Activities funded research in the summer of 1997 that was helpful in preparing for the SVU conference and subsequent book project.

TEXAS COUNTIES WITH SPJST LODGES IN 1897.

The SPJST began operation in 1897 with twenty-five charter lodges, located in thirteen Texas counties. Six of the lodges were located in Fayette County (Fayetteville, La Grange, Ammansville, Praha, Dubina, Engle); six in Lavaca County (Novohrad, Hallettsville, Shiner, Bila Hora, Moravia, Velehrad); three in Burleson County (Caldwell, Snook, Novy Tabor); and one each in McLennan (Cottonwood), Colorado (Weimar), Lee (Dime Box), Washington (Veseli, later "Wesley"), Milam (Bucholts), Bastrop (Elgin), Williamson (Granger), Austin (Cat Spring), Bell (Cyclone), and Ellis (Ennis) Counties.

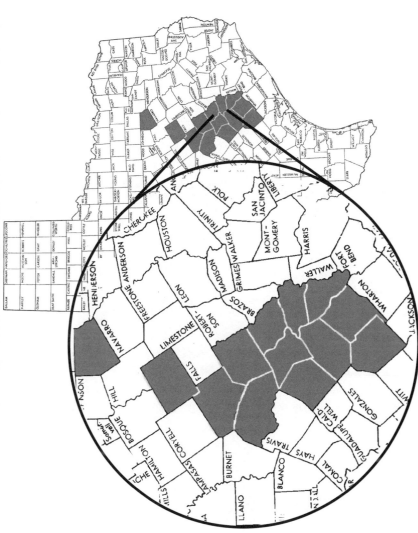

— Map courtesy of the *Texas Almanac*

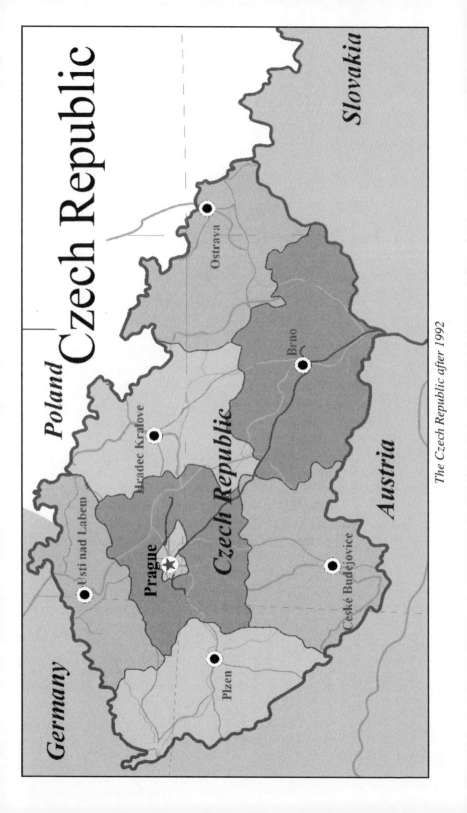

The Czech Republic after 1992

The Czech Ambassador's Address on the Occasion of the 100th Anniversary of the SPJST

Alexandr Vondra

Dear President Leshikar, Ladies and Gentlemen, Dear Friends, *milí přátelé*! Thank you for your invitation and the opportunity to speak before you during the celebration of the 100th anniversary of the founding of the SPJST.

Allow me to express my best wishes to the *Slovanská podporující jednota statu Texas* on behalf of President Václav Havel as well as on behalf of the Government of the Czech Republic. Let me assure you that this event is followed with great respect in my country. It is my pleasure to read here a greeting that President Václav Havel sent to you:

Dear Mr. Leshikar, Dear Mr. Rechcígl,

Allow me to use this opportunity to greet all the participants of the 100th anniversary celebration of the SPJST (*Slovanská podporující jednota statu Texas*). Even though my official state duties preclude me from being with you, I shall follow your activities and their results with great interest.

I am pleased that this tradition of gatherings of people with Czech ancestry in Texas continues and thus builds on the rich heritage of cultural and social activities of the Czech American community in the United States.

I am glad that you maintain a close relationship with the

country of origin of your forefathers, and I wish all participants
of the gathering in Belton much success for the future as well.

— Václav Havel

Texas is a beautiful state. The majestic beauty of its nature
was buttressed by the efforts of your ancestors, who came to the
United States with their hopes and dreams. They were looking for
a better life, with religious freedom, and they had a desire to help
build this wonderful country.

There is a terrific history of Czech-Americans, and of the
Czech Texans, with heroes like Lešikar, Šilar, and Bergman. They
were the pioneers of the path from Bohemia and Moravia to Texas.
They were not afraid of hard work or dissuaded by the dangers of
crossing the Atlantic. They came to seek the chance of their lives.
And we all know that they used this opportunity to the fullest.

On their journey away from poverty, there were things which
united them and gave them the power to face new challenges. It
was the common bond with the old homeland and the relatives
they had to leave behind. It was the joint hardship that they all had
to face to build a better life. Most of all, it was their trust in God
and in a brighter future. Farming to them wasn't just a way of making a living. It was their identity, a way of life. You have gathered
here today to honor their struggle and to celebrate the hardy Czech
folks who were your forebears. This is something your old country
can also be proud of.

One of my favorite goals in the U.S. is to support and help
develop the Czech and Moravian spirit in America. As I see you
all here today, it seems to me that the Czech spirit in Texas is
doing quite well. Your presence makes me remember the words of
the great Czech Vojta Náprstek: "That which the heart unites, the
sea shall not divide." I have already heard about all the famous
Czech and Slovak festivals being organized, like the festival in
West, and the National Polka Festival; and I look forward to the
day when I will be able to pay a visit to all these festivities, to say
"Thank you" to all of you who have guarded the Czech heritage
throughout the years.

Czech-American relations are reaching a new level now. With
the Czechs in America and the Czechs at home, I know that there
are certain problems that must be solved. But I also believe that

the existence of a problem in itself is not as important as the will to solve it. I want to assure you that I and my Government share this will and commitment.

Recently, the Czech Republic has had to confront a historic challenge. After the dark years of Communism, we had to rebuild our lives and our country from scratch. We have finally made true our dream of living under a government of our own choice, and we managed to erase the artificial dividing line in Europe which was drawn at the end of World War II.

America is a country that supported the former Czechoslovakia from its cradle. It also sacrificed much for peace and stability in Europe over the last several decades. You as American citizens contributed to this effort with your daily work. American citizens are the sturdy pillar that makes America so strong. I am really proud that some of the citizens who make this society strong and healthy are of Czech origin. America serves as a wonderful example that sustaining a society of freedom and happiness is a permanent task requiring constant vigilance.

I also hear that many of you were involved in the U.S. armed forces in defense of peace and democracy throughout this century. Allow me to use this opportunity to thank you for your courage and heroism. Certainly, one of these successful peace-keeping missions brought liberty to the Czechoslovakian people in 1945.

We are here today to celebrate the 100th anniversary of the SPJST. Its ideal of fraternalism helped the people survive the most difficult times of their lives. It was formed upon the principle that man is indeed his brother's keeper and that each of us is responsible for his fellow man. The spirit of the Brotherhood of Man stimulated the development of different fraternal organizations throughout history. In a time when insurance was a luxury available to only a few, the fraternal system made it possible to launch a program that could provide working members with protection for their dependents. After almost fifty years, the struggle for the best possible structure culminated in the founding of the SPJST in 1897.

One of the principles the SPJST was built on was "togetherness," to make life more enjoyable and to protect one another. This is very similar to the principle of collective defense which brought stability in transatlantic areas to countries which share the same values and ideals in Europe and in America.

The Czech Republic was born just a few years ago. It has grown up fast, and it is now ready to share the responsibility for the future prosperity and stability of Europe. We are prepared to carry this cross, and we know that you, the Czech-Americans, vowing with us never to repeat the past, will stand by our side.

I came back from the NATO Summit in Madrid just a few days ago. It was a unique conference. It was one of the moments when history is made. The ghosts of Munich and Yalta, the ghosts of Communism and Soviet expansion, are gone. America and Europe are here today to develop a true cooperation and partnership to safeguard liberty, freedom, and a common heritage. NATO is a pillar in this achievement, and the Czech Republic will be a part of it.

We hope that you will be proud of us as much as we are proud of you, and that you will support our will to protect our common values. I believe that my presence here is the beginning of a new relationship between you and the people representing the Czech Republic both in the U.S. and at home.

I wanted to stay here with you for the whole meeting. Unfortunately, I have to leave earlier. I am going to Prague on the occasion of Secretary Albright's visit. I think you agree with me that Madeleine Albright is one of the Czech-Americans we can really be proud of. I can assure you, however, that my heart will stay here with you for the rest of your celebrations.

I wish you every possible success. Thank you, and God bless you. *Bůh Vám žehnej. Na shledanou.*

The Czech Republic and Czechs Abroad: Past, Present, and Future

Zdeněk Lyčka

The Czech Republic is a very young state — it has existed for just four and a half years — but it was established on the historical territory of the Czech Crown that already was on the map of Central Europe a thousand years ago. Nevertheless, during these thousand years of existence, Czechs — like many other European nations — could not live in peace and many of them had to emigrate.

At present, the total number of Czechs and persons of Czech descent residing permanently abroad is about 2.2 million. The largest community lives in the U.S. (about 1.3 million). Other large communities are in Slovakia (60,000); Canada (56,000); Germany (46,000); Austria (30,000); Australia (20,000-30,000); Croatia (13,000); and Switzerland (9,000). Smaller numbers live in other West-European countries, South America, South Africa, and Asia. Czech emigrants in East-European countries are almost exclusively the descendants of pre-war emigrants, some of them as early as the eighteenth century.

The Ministry of Foreign Affairs of the Czech Republic has contacts with more than 280 organizations of Czechs living abroad and friends of the Czech Republic all over the world (most of them in the U.S.). They regularly publish dozens of periodicals:

some of them distributed only to members, others (especially in the U.S., Canada, and Australia) addressing all Czechs living in the country and even the general public in the Czech Republic.

The Attitude of the Czech State toward Czechs Abroad

Shortly after the establishment of the Czechoslovak Republic, emigration issues were administered by the Ministry of Social Affairs. These issues were also dealt with, however, by the so-called Emigration Institute of the Masaryk Academy of Labor and the Ministry of Foreign Affairs.

The most significant organization in this field was established in 1928 as the Czechoslovak Foreign Institute, which assumed an active role mainly in meeting the cultural and educational requirements of Czechs and Slovaks living abroad, though its resources were limited. The Institute published a monthly magazine called *Krajan*, organized the sending of teachers to help Czech and Slovak communities abroad, and, above all, provided valuable information to potential emigrants about the countries they had decided to live in.

The outbreak of the economic crisis at the end of the 1920s caused the establishment of the Czechoslovak Colonization Society, which assumed the task of mass colonization focused on farm workers. For those leaving the country, emigration posts in Praha-Libeň and in Svatobořice near Brno were established.

From the beginning of the 1930s, the so-called Masaryk Days of Czechoslovaks Abroad were organized with the aim of keeping the public informed of the Czechs and Slovaks living abroad and their importance for the country. It was only the German occupation of the country that put the final end to this tradition. The frontiers were sealed, and the Protectorate authorities made further emigration practically impossible.

With the totalitarian takeover in Czechoslovakia in February 1948, the position of the state towards emigrants changed completely: leaving the country illegally began to be considered a crime (until then it was regarded merely as a minor offence and exceptionally as a violation of the military service law). Criminal proceedings were started against nearly all who had left the country. At the same time the Communist regime started to establish cooperation with selected "loyal" societies, thereby causing tension among the exiles. Further steps were taken in the 1970s when the regime allowed the so-called regulation of relations with the Czechoslovak Socialist Republic (the emigrants were allowed to "redeem" themselves from the "sin" of emigration). Many people accepted this and could visit their relatives in Czechoslovakia. At the same time criminal proceedings against these emigrants were abated.

Matters related to Czechs and Slovaks living abroad were administered by the Czechoslovak Foreign Institute, which until 1989 constituted the only government platform in the country in this field as it was part of the Federal Ministry of Foreign Affairs. The Institute's material support—as well as support in the form of sending folklore specialists, film and theatre directors, and sports delegations, and enabling Czechs and Slovaks living abroad to participate in language courses in the country, etc.—was, however, oriented towards societies developing no political activities and focusing only on preserving old traditions, or those in which the Communist state was politically interested. After 1989, when the Institute became independent of the Foreign Ministry and became a civic organization, focusing on civil and property matters and providing consultations concerning Czechs and Slovaks living abroad, there existed no specialized state body dealing with Czechs and Slovaks living abroad.

It was only in May 1992 that the Government passed Decision 375, by which relations with Czechs and Slovaks living abroad became part of the activities of the Center for Non-Governmental Relations of the Federal Ministry of Foreign Affairs. After the constitution of the independent Czech Republic, the Center was transformed into the Department for Relations with Czechs Living Abroad and for Non-Governmental Relations. The Department existed from March 1, 1993, until April 21, 1997, when it merged with the former Department for Cultural and Scientific Relations and was renamed the Department for Cultural Relations and Czechs Living Abroad (OKKV).

The top-level authorities dealing with problems of Czechs living abroad are currently the Sub-Committee for Czechs Living

Abroad of the Foreign Relations Committee of the Chamber of Deputies of the Parliament of the Czech Republic and the recently established Standing Commission of the Senate for Czechs Living Abroad.

Apart from the OKKV and the Parliament, these matters are dealt with also by certain non-governmental organizations, such as the already mentioned Czechoslovak Institute for Foreign Relations, occasionally by the International Czech Club, and others. Scientific studies of emigration and studies of problems of Czechs living abroad are centered in the Institute of Ethnography and Folklorism of the Czech Academy of Sciences in Prague, the Náprstek Museum (and the Museum of Czechs and Slovaks Living Abroad, associated with it in 1938), the Czechoslovak Center for Exiles Studies of Palacký University in Olomouc, and other institutions.

Department for Cultural Relations and Czechs Living Abroad (OKKV)

As one of the successor states of the Czech and Slovak Federal Republic, the Czech Republic proceeds, in developing relations with Czechs living abroad, from the principles adopted by the Government of the Czech and Slovak Federal Republic on May 21, 1992. These principles formulate the government policy pursued in respect of Czechs abroad as follows:

a) to maintain permanent information links, possibly also a dialogue on such government policy issues that may touch the interests of Czechs living abroad;
b) to preserve and develop the cultural, language and historical feeling of belonging to their old homeland;
c) to create such conditions in the economic field that will permit Czechs living abroad to help the Czech and Slovak Federal Republic (the Czech Republic) in its further development or — on the other hand — to develop suitable forms of helping these people if they are in need.

In bilateral relations towards countries with larger Czech communities, the Czech Republic has been trying to provide favorable conditions for the support of such communities by the partner state. This approach is, however, not based on the principle of reciprocity, an example of which is the publication of printed matters for national minorities in the Czech Republic in the Slovak, Polish, German, and Romany languages, paid for by the Czech government.

The main objective of the Ministry of Foreign Affairs is to help the communities showing interest in maintaining cultural, language, and historical links with the old homeland. The future of many societies of Czechs living abroad can be seen in supporting their gradual opening to the majority population, and their transformation into "Societies of Friends of the Czech Republic." Compared to the situation before 1989, the so-called loyalty and usefulness of a community, society or individual for the political purposes of the country are now no longer decisive for the extent of support provided to them. In short, the Department for Cultural Relations and Czechs Living Abroad (OKKV) plays its role above all in the field of information, assistance, and cultural promotion.

At this point we must admit that it was, and sometimes still is, lack of information that hinders the development of mutual contacts and a more active approach to some societies or communities. In an effort to improve this situation, the OKKV has taken two important steps:

a) It started to publish *Information for Czechs Living Abroad,* a bulletin appearing twice a year that provides information in the legal, educational, and cultural fields, such as the availability of Czech language courses and study stays, books, CDs, and audio and video cassettes. Our Department can provide this publication to the societies free of charge. (Any remarks concerning the contents of the bulletin will be much appreciated.)

b) Our Department has also begun to build its own information database containing the lists of all societies and organizations, prominent Czechs living abroad, data on communities' libraries and archives, and publications—as well as data—on supportive activities of the OKKV. The Department has put together a comprehensive questionnaire that was sent to all societies, hoping they will help complete the database, which serves the internal needs of the Department. Unfortunately, in many cases, the Department is not informed about the activities of individual societies, or the information arrives belatedly, sometimes even after an event is already over, and sometimes the Department is not informed at all. It is then impossible to inform the Czech public of such events or to support them. The gathering of information on Czech communities, societies, or personalities living abroad, and their activities and expectations in respect to the Czech Republic, is aimed at intensifying active assistance to Czechs living abroad by the Czech Republic.

Apart from this, the Department develops cooperation with the Foreign Service of Czech Radio, which is ready to prepare special programs at the request of Czech communities' radio stations, in addition to its regular services.

The most important activities of the Department undoubtedly include providing various kinds of materials in the field of culture and promotion, such as books, textbooks, periodicals, phonographs, and videocassettes to societies, schools, or editors, either on the basis of their specific requests or in the form of financial contributions to individual projects.

In 1996 alone, the Ministry of Foreign Affairs spent about 11 million Czech crowns on these forms of projects and about the same amount is earmarked for this year (1997).

Our Department initiated programs of assistance in the field of education: the sending of teachers, Czech language courses and study stays in the Czech Republic for teachers who will be teaching the Czech language in Czech communities abroad, and other like exchanges. The programs are prepared and carried out in close cooperation with the Ministry of Education and are becoming very popular. For example, this year interest in Czech language courses exceeded our capacity by more than 100 per cent. Several teachers have been sent for the first time to Czech communities, e.g., in Australia and Croatia. This again, however, requires intensive cooperation on the part of these societies and communities.

The Department also participates in projects of technical assistance, such as the reconstruction of Czech schools and cultural centers of Czechs living abroad. In 1996, the Czech government earmarked certain amounts for the repair of schools, cultural centers, and roads in areas inhabited by Czech communities in Romania; the repair of the Comenius school in Vienna (the largest of its kind in the world); the repair of the Comenius Mausoleum in Naarden, Holland; and the maintenance of the Museum of Emigrants in Zelów, Poland.

The basic condition, often very demanding, for the realization of such projects, is effective cooperation and coordination between the Ministry of Foreign Affairs and individual societies, to ensure the technical preparation of projects and their completion.

The OKKV is also doing its best to meet the requests of Czechs living abroad concerning legal and political matters. It thoroughly and continuously has been monitoring problems, particularly those concerning exiles. One of the latest activities in this respect is the analysis of the problem of citizenship of Czechs living abroad, and the possibility of exercising the right to vote abroad by those who have Czech citizenship. In this respect, the OKKV has been intensifying cooperation with both the Chamber of Deputies and the Senate of the Parliament of the Czech Republic.

The Department is well aware that, given its personnel and financial capacities, it cannot meet all the requests and needs of the more than three hundred societies and organizations of Czechs living abroad, and friends of the Czech Republic, as well as a great number of Czech non-governmental organizations.

The Future

The activities developed by Czechs living abroad—ranging from the period of the post-White Mountain exiles to the emigration waves of the past several decades—constitute an important part of the Czech national and cultural heritage. Preserving this heritage is one of the ways of increasing the credibility of the Czech Republic as an advanced cultural country, as well as a contribution to the development of bilateral relations with countries where Czech communities have been living. In this context we would appreciate the help provided by some societies of Czechs living abroad, or by individuals, in promoting the image of the Czech Republic. And here I would like to thank especially American Friends of the Czech Republic and the Czech and Slovak Solidarity Council, as well as the SVU, for their support as far as the entrance of the Czech Republic into NATO is concerned.

Despite certain remaining problems, we can state that the scope of communication and cooperation between the Czech Republic and Czechs living abroad has been deepening. The OKKV welcomes all initiatives and suggestions enhancing the development between the Czech Republic and Czechs living abroad and especially an intensified exchange of information. Representatives of societies as well as individual visitors are most welcome to come and see us at our Department.

A Brief History
of the SPJST

Leonard D. Mikeska

Mr. Ambassador, Alexandr Vondra, and distinguished guests from the Czech Republic, esteemed leaders, and members of the SVU. I am very pleased that we have been able to blend your SVU Conference with the SPJST Centennial activities. Thank you for the opportunity to share some brief highlights in the history of the SPJST.

The SPJST began operation on July 1, 1897, after the major organizational plan had been worked out at a convention the month before. We began operation with twenty-five lodges and 782 members. The organization was known as the *Slovanská podporující jednota státu Texas*. Over the years, we became known best by the initials "SPJST." Later, our corporate name was translated into English and the charter amended to reflect this change. The English translation is Slavonic Benevolent Order of the State of Texas (SPJST).

By 1900 many people of Czech descent had immigrated to the United States, especially from the Czech lands of Moravia, Bohemia, and Slovakia. They sought freedom and opportunity, and many chose Texas as their new home.

In the 1880s many of the Czech immigrants to Texas took membership in the nationwide fraternal organization known as the

13

Česko-slovánská podporující společnost, the ČSPS. In 1896, a dispute arose between the Texas ČSPS delegation and the nation-wide organization over what were thought by the Texans to be high premiums. This dispute was one of the factors that led to the organization of the SPJST. Three individuals who were highly instrumental in either organizing or promoting the new SPJST were I. J. Gallia, the first president; J. R. Kubena, the first secretary; and Augustin Haidušek, a prominent pioneer and backer of the SPJST.

During the early years of my employment with the SPJST in the late 1950s, I recall a number of senior members who relished sharing their recollections about the early years of the SPJST. They spoke of the needs that were met in very real human terms. For instance, how the SPJST lodges rallied the Czech immigrants together to learn to cope with the challenges of settling our state. They spoke of countless acts of benevolent assistance and charitable acts within the communities, and how these pioneers assisted one another. The SPJST lodges also served as the focal point that brought people together for social and cultural sustenance. These people saw the importance of death benefits for the sake of widows and children of deceased members.

During the first forty years of its existence, the affairs of the SPJST were handled in the back room of the general merchandise store of Secretary J. R. Kuběna in Fayetteville, Texas. After Kuběna's death in 1938, the Society rented office space in Fayetteville for its growing operation. The 1930s saw the Society take in additional full time officers. The 1952 convention in Houston decided to move the Society headquarters to Temple, Texas, to a six-story office building acquired to serve as a Home Office for the Supreme Lodge. The move was accomplished in 1953. On January 31, 1971, the Society moved into a new Home Office which included an extensive library, archives, and museum.

As the organization grew, many areas developed and added to the character and influence of the Society. I will mention some of them.

Lodge Halls

The SPJST has a network of 112 lodges in various com-

munities throughout Texas. Many of the lodges own their buildings. These buildings have always been locally owned and con-
trolled. The first of our lodge halls were simple structures, in many
cases constructed cooperatively by the members themselves. The
construction of lodge halls continued until recent times, with
many modern lodge homes now in place. Lodge halls tend to be
focal points in individual communities. They bring people together and sustain activities that help preserve our Czech culture
and heritage.

Life Insurance Benefits

One of the original purposes for organizing the Society was
the need to provide financial benefits to widows and children.
From the meager beginnings of an assessment system of death
benefits, the SPJST developed into a legal reserve Fraternal Life
Insurance Company. From very simple beginnings, the complexity
of insurance now necessitates a portfolio of products to meet a
variety of needs in providing economic security for families.

Youth Activities

In the early fifties, leaders in the organization saw the need to
prepare our youth for future leadership roles. A Youth Department
began to develop, one which would involve youth throughout the
State. We now have separate youth clubs in many lodges, a summer camp program, leader training programs, and two major
statewide activity days. The '80s also saw the development of a
scholarship program. The organization's focus on young people
has helped us grow and retain our strength.

Věstník

Since 1912 the Society has published *Věstník*, a weekly journal. *Věstník* provided the communication to bring the organization
together. The Czech section no doubt had a significant impact on

preserving the Czech language. Communication through *Věstník* reinforced our people's sense of ownership and participation in the Society.

Library, Archives and Museum (LAM)

At the 1968 SPJST Convention, a commitment was made to develop a LAM department. Since that time, the Society has received numerous artifacts and an assortment of collectibles and antique items. The library now contains over 18,000 books in the Czech language. The LAM also contains a vast assortment of historical and genealogical information. The LAM is located at SPJST headquarters in Temple, Texas.

The SPJST: Shaping and Preserving a Heritage

Visitors from the Czech Republic often express surprise in finding third and fourth generation descendants of Czech immigrants who still have pride in their heritage. Although some families have been in America almost 140 years, a significant number of the grandchildren and great-grandchildren of those immigrants still speak the Czech language. The SPJST has served to keep alive customs, traditions, and a sense of pride in their roots. The SPJST has had a profound impact on Czech-American relations. The majority of Czech immigrants holding membership in the SPJST were farmers. Prior to mid-century, they and their children began to move to the cities in large numbers. The SPJST moved with them to the cities and was crucial to maintaining their ethnic connection.

The SPJST has served to bring people together, and we have been shaped by the people we have served. The SPJST had no religious affiliation, a fact which opened the organization to a variety of influences. The organization brought people of different religious affiliations together to work side by side in our ranks. I think that this factor had a unifying influence on our people and served to foster a beautiful spirit of understanding and cooperation.

Anyone desiring to do more research on the history of the SPJST is directed to *A History of the SPJST*, compiled by Nick A. Morris. You are also directed to "The SPJST Centennial Extra" appearing in the July 6, 1997, edition of the *Temple Daily Telegram*. The back issues of the *Věstník* in our Archives are also replete with detailed historical information.

After one hundred years, the culture and heritage of this organization is alive and well. There is much enthusiasm which we know will motivate our leaders to seek out new ways to meet the needs of our people. Our leadership is of one mind that "the best is yet to come."

Thank you very much.

Bohemian and Moravian Pioneers in Colonial America*

Miloslav Rechcígl, Jr.

Although a major exodus of Czechs to America did not take place until after the revolutionary year of 1848, there is plenty of evidence on hand attesting to numerous cases of individual migrations from the Czech lands not too long after the New World was discovered.

As surprising as it may sound to the readers of this essay, according to some scholars, Czechs could actually claim some credit for the discovery of the New World. I am referring to German author Franz Loeher[1] who made the claim that Martin Behaim, rather than Columbus, or for that matter Amerigo Vespucci, was the true discoverer of America. Loeher celebrates Behaim, whom he considers to be a German, not only as the first European to view the coast of America off Brazil in the year 1483, but also as the instructor in western navigation of both of the putative later discoverers and explorers, Columbus and Magellan. Although Loeher's claim was later disputed, and even ridiculed, Behaim was known to have taken part in the expedition of Diego

---

* This paper is based, in part, on my study "In the Footprints of the First Czech Immigrants in America," *Czechoslovak and Central European Journal,* vol. 9 (1990), pp. 75-90.

Cap (1485-1486) that followed the coast of Africa to Cape Cross. His most important work, which places him among the greatest geographers of the Renaissance, was his terrestrial globe, the earliest one extant, which has been preserved in Nuremberg. What role this globe played in the actual discovery of the New World is not known. As the name indicates, Behaim was not a German at all but rather a Bohemian. The name Behaim is the old German equivalent of the later used term Boehme (i.e. Bohemian) which, prior to the usage of family surnames, was commonly used to designate individuals coming from Bohemia or the Czech lands. According to family tradition, the Behaim family moved to Nuremberg from Bohemia after the death of the Czech Duke Vratislav I.[2]

Be that as it may, the news of the discovery of the New World reached the Kingdom of Bohemia as early as the first decade of the sixteenth century, during the reign of Vladislav the Jagellonian (1471-1516). Proof of this is given by the existence of an early print in the Czech language, *Spis o nowých zemiech a o nowem swietie o niemžto jsme prwe žadne znamosti nemeli ani kdy tzo slychali*, the origin of which has been placed at about 1509. It is an adaptation of the renowned letter of Amerigo Vespucci addressed to the Medici family, appended with other texts. The Czech version apparently preceded those of other European nations in this regard since, other than the Czech version, only the Latin original exists from that period. The printer and publisher of this rare print is purported to be Mikuláš Bakalář, originally Štětina, of Pilsen, Bohemia.[3]

The first visitors from the Czech lands to the New World were an anonymous group of miners from Jáchymov, Bohemia who, prior to 1528, were sent to Little Naples (present Venezuela) to establish the silver mines in that country, while in the employ of the banking house of the Walser family.[4] The project apparently ended in failure since, after a short time, the Walsers gave up their efforts of mining silver there, and the miners returned home. We also have a record from that period regarding a Moravian jeweler in Mexico who was accused in 1536 of heresy and sentenced to do public penance and expulsion from the Spanish territory.[5]

The first documented case of the entry of a Bohemian on the North American shores is that of Joachim Gans of Prague who came to what is now Roanoke, North Carolina, in 1585 with an expedition of explorers, organized by Sir Walter Raleigh (1552-1618) and commanded by Raleigh's cousin Sir Richard Greenville (1542-1591). It is noteworthy that this expedition originated from Plymouth, England, thirty years before the Pilgrims set sail from the same port on their historic voyage to America. Due to lack of provisions for the colonists, and the inherent dangers from the Spaniards and the Indians, the expedition had to be abruptly called to an end on June 19, 1856, when Sir Francis Drake (1516-1590) was asked to take the whole company of colonists back to England.[6]

Who the first permanent Czech settler in America was, we cannot say with certainty. It is certain, however, that among the first was the famed Augustine Herman (1621-1686) from Prague. He was a surveyor and skilled draftsman, successful planter and developer of new lands, a shrewd and enterprising merchant, a bold politician, an effective diplomat, and fluent in several languages — clearly one of the most conspicuous and colorful personalities of seventeenth-century colonial America. After coming to New Amsterdam (present New York) he became one of the most influential people in the Dutch Province, which led to his appointment to the Council of Nine to advise the New Amsterdam Governor. One of his greatest achievements was his celebrated map of Maryland and Virginia commissioned by Lord Baltimore on which he began working in earnest after removing to the English Province of Maryland. Lord Baltimore was so pleased with the map, that he rewarded Herman with a large estate, named by Herman "Bohemia Manor," as well as the hereditary title Lord.[7]

There was another Bohemian living in New Amsterdam at that time: Frederick Philipse (1626-1720), who became equally famous in his own right. He was a successful merchant who eventually became the wealthiest person in the entire Dutch Province. He was descended from an aristocratic Protestant family from Bohemia, who had to flee from their native land at the outbreak of the Thirty Years' War.[8]

Preserved records document that other natives of the Czech lands lived in New Amsterdam, some of whom may have been there even prior to the arrival of Augustine Herman and Frederick Philipse. One can find in the archives of the Reformed Dutch

Church the record of a marriage between a Moravian by name of J. Fradel with a Tyn Hersker. The ceremony took place in February 1645. Several other Czech sounding names appear in the Dutch records, including those of Hollar, Adam Unkelbe, John Kostlo, and Loketka. There is also evidence of the presence of Czechs in Virginia, as attested by early ship passenger lists. Czech names also appear in some documents in Massachusetts and Connecticut. Signs of early Czech presence can also be found in parish records in Barbados, as evidenced by such names as Richard Benes, Anthony Slany, or John Hudlice.[9]

During the anti-reformation period, while the Czech Protestants in Bohemia, Moravia, and Silesia were undergoing their greatest persecution, the Czech Jesuits took the initiative of launching their extraordinarily ambitious, world-wide missionary effort among Indians, Filipinos, Chinese, and Ethiopians. The Bohemian Province of the Society of Jesus sent 160 of its members overseas, including thirty-six to Mexico, three to Lower California (now a part of Mexico), three to New Granada (present Venezuela), seventeen to Ecuador, seventeen to Peru, twenty-six to Paraguay, twelve to Chile, nine to China, seven to Annam (present Vietnam), four to Goa, and two to the coast of Malabar. Half were clergymen, and half were lay brethren, trained in some trade or craft.[10]

Valentin Stansel (1621-1705) was apparently the first Jesuit who worked in Latin America. After joining the Jesuit Order, he became a professor of rhetoric and mathematics in Olomouc, Moravia, and later in Prague. After ordination he opted for missionary work in India, then left for Portugal, where he awaited the arrival of a ship. In the meantime he taught astronomy at the university in Evora. When his trip to India did not materialize, he was sent in 1657 to Brazil and taught at the Jesuit College and Seminary in Bahia (present Salvador). First he held the position of a professor of moral theology and later was promoted to a chancellor. In addition to his teaching career, he also conducted research in astronomy and made a number of important discoveries, especially of comets. Some of his observations were subsequently published in Prague, under the title *Observationes Americanae Cometae.*

A steady stream of missionaries began leaving for Latin

America soon after the *Bohemian Societatis Jesu* was admitted for the missionary work there in 1644. Among the first missionaries selected were Matiáš Kukulin from Mohelnice, Moravia; Václav Christmann from Prague; Pavel Klein from Cheb, Bohemia; Josef Neumann from Olomouc, Moravia; Augustin Strobach from Jihlava, Moravia; and Jan Tilpe from Silesia. Later on, the group was joined by Brother Šimon Boruhradský from Polná, Bohemia. In June 1678 the group left Genoa, Italy, and from there they sailed to Portugal. They were beset with difficulties from the start. One vessel, with numerous missionaries on board, was wrecked immediately after setting sail, and the voyagers barely escaped with their lives. Only a few missionaries succeeded in persuading the captain of the ship *San Ignacio* to take them on board. After many difficulties they finally arrived in October 1680 in Mexico City, the capital city of New Spain. Christmann remained in Latin America until the end of his life (1723) and spent most of that time in Paraguay. Klein later left for the Philippine Islands. Both Tilpe and Strobach removed to the Pacific coast and sailed to the Mariana Islands where they met Kukulin. Neumann and Boruhradský remained in Mexico.

The second group of Czech Jesuits began their journey to Latin America in 1684, their destination being Peru and Chile. The group included Jiří Burger, Ignat Fritz, and Václav Richter from Moravia. Jiří Brand and Ondřej Supetius came from Silesia. They were followed by other groups destined for New Granada (present Columbia), Venezuela, Brazil, and other countries in Latin America, in order to broaden their missionary work.

Among these missionaries, Šimon Boruhradský will be remembered forever in Mexican history for his melioration structures that saved several cities from devastating floods, and his part in the rebuilding of the vice-regent's palace after it was burned down by Indians. Jiří Hostinský from Valašské Klobouky was an outstanding authority on Indian dialects who demonstrated his abilities during the negotiations with Indians of the powerful Tarahumara tribe. Josef Neumann is credited with writing the history of the tribe's uprising, while Matěj Steffel compiled a dictionary of their language. Adam Gilig of Rýmařov, Moravia did the same with reference to the dialects of the Pinas and Eudeve tribes.

In the region of today's Venezuela several Czech missionaries excelled, including Vojtěch Bukovský, a scion of an old family of Bohemian Knights of Hustiřany, Bohemia, Jindřich Václav Richter from Prostějov, Moravia, and Samuel Fritz from Trutnov, Bohemia. Fritz succeeded in converting, among others, the powerful tribe of Omaguas and concentrating into civilized settlements the natives of forty different localities. Adept in technical arts and handicraft, he was also endowed with extraordinary linguistic abilities, supplemented by the rare gift of knowing intuitively how to treat the Indians. In 1689 he undertook, in primitive Parakou, a daring expedition down the Amazon to Para, where he was captured and imprisoned for two years on the suspicion of being a Spanish spy. Although only imperfectly equipped with the necessary instruments, he completed a relatively accurate chart of the river's course. This was the first such attempt to chart the Maranon territory.

Among the Czech missionaries in Peru who excelled were Stanislav Arlet from Silesia, the founder of San Pedro, and František Boryně from Lhota, Bohemia. According to his contemporaries, Boryně worked more effectively than twenty missionaries, converting to Christianity over 100 different tribes. He founded a whole series of new posts, built beautiful churches, introduced new agricultural practices and trades, taught native women how to spin flax and men how to weave. Brother Jan Roehr from Prague was responsible for preparing the architectural plans of the famed cathedral in Lima, after its destruction by the earthquake of 1746. František Eder of Kremnice will be remembered for writing an authoritative account of the hard and distressful life in the Majos Mission where the missionaries resembled "living corpses" rather than human beings.

Jiří Burger from Vískov in Moravia served in the Chilean province. His Spanish excelled that of most native speakers. In 1700 he was put in charge of the College in Chillan. Father Supetius from Silesia, who held the position of chancellor of the Jesuit College in Santiago, wrote with pride in one of his letters, "All of us who came here from the Bohemian Province can truthfully confirm that the native Fathers in Chile of Spanish parentage love and hold in high esteem the Czechs above all other nations, even above European Spaniards, which is among these people extremely rare . . ." Jan Josef Čermák from Moravské Budějovice and Václav Horský from Hrádec Králové deserve mention among the Czechs serving here.

It is of note that the Czech missionaries participated in the rebuilding of the Jesuit state of Paraguay, called by Voltaire a "victory of humanity," even though he was a deadly enemy of the Jesuits. A number of Czechs were active here, including Václav Christmann from Prague; Jan John from Jaroměř; and Jindřich Kordule from Bestvina.

This narrative hardly touches on the varied activities of Czech missionaries in Latin America, nor does it do justice to the hardships, stress, and the inhumane conditions under which they had to live—impenetrable jungles, the most severe climatic conditions, incurable diseases; not to mention frequent hunger and constant danger from wild Indians.

The first significant wave of Czech colonists to come to America was that of the Moravian Brethren, who began arriving on the American shores in the first half of the eighteenth century. Moravian Brethren were the followers of the teachings of the Czech religious reformer and martyr Jan Hus (1370-1415) and John Amos Comenius (1592-1670).[11] They were the true heirs of the ancient *Unitas fratrum bohemicorum*, who found a temporary refuge in Herrnhut ("*Ochranov*," in the Czech language) in Lusatia under the patronage of Count Nikolaus Zinzendorf (1700-1760). Because of the worsening political and religious situation in Saxony, the Moravian Brethren, as they had begun to call themselves, had to seek a more permanent home and a new territory where they could freely profess their faith and expand their mission activities. The North American continent, with its abundance of fertile land and large Indian population, was ideally suited for their aims. After initial visits to St. Thomas in 1732, and Greenland in 1733, ten selected Brethren sailed in November 1734 to the English province of Georgia, arriving in Savannah in February 1735. In the summer of the same year a second group, under the leadership of Bishop David Nitschmann, followed. This group comprised twenty-five persons, the majority of whom were from Moravia or Bohemia. Among the passengers on the ship was John Wesley (1703-1791), the founder of the Methodist Church, who became acquainted with the Brethren, attended their services, worshipped with them, and lived in their homes during his initial stay in Georgia. Through the efforts of Bishop Nitschmann, the Brethren were soon organized into a congregation. Brother Anton Seiffert, a native of Bohemia, was ordained as their preacher and named their elder. In 1736 they built the first church of Moravian Brethren in North America. Despite their efforts, the Moravians did not find Georgia adequate for their religious pursuits, and in 1740 the majority decided to leave for Pennsylvania, which offered better conditions.

The third group of Moravian settlers, called by early Moravian historians "The First Sea Congregation," arrived in Philadelphia in June 1742. The largest contingent of Moravian Brethren ever to come to America arrived May 17, 1749, in New York. With the John Nitschmann Colony, came Christian David of Ženklava, Moravia, the founder of Brethren's Herrnhut, and Matthew and Rosina Stach, Moravian missionaries in Greenland.

The ranking place among the early Moravians was held by Bishop Daniel Nitschmann (1691-1749), a native of Suchdol, Moravia, who devoted his entire life to the Moravian Church. He had fled in 1724 to Herrnhut and was immediately engaged in evangelic work in Germany and Russia. In 1732 he went, together with Leupold Dober, to St. Thomas, Virgin Islands, as the first Moravian missionaries "among the heathens." In 1735 he was consecrated the first bishop of the renewed Unity by Bishop Jablonsky of Berlin, the grandson of the famed John Amos Comenius, thus assuring the continuation of the evangelic work of the ancient *Unitas fratrum* of Bohemian Brethren. The following year he led the Moravian colony to Georgia. In 1740 he came to Pennsylvania. In 1743 he purchased a track of land on the Lehigh River where he founded a small colony, from the abandoned settlement in Georgia, which he named Bethlehem. In 1744 he returned to Saxony but later extended his labors to New York and North Carolina. During his lifetime he visited the principal countries of Northern Europe and the West Indies, making close to fifty sea voyages. In 1755 he returned to Pennsylvania and resided in Weissport and Lititz, and later at Bethlehem.

Thanks to the foresight and historical sense of George Neisser (1715-1784) from Žilina, Moravia, we have a detailed account of the early events in Bethlehem, as well as Moravian Church history during the formative years. Rev. George Neisser was the first archivist and diarist of Bethlehem. He was also the first schoolmaster and postmaster. Nathaniel Seidel (1718-1782), a descendant of Bohemian emigrants from Silesia, served for twenty years as the president of the American Provincial Board of the Elders.

David Zeisberger, Jr, whose parents forsook their considerable estate in Moravia and fled for conscience's sake to Herrnhut, after coming to America in 1738, embarked on an intensive study of Indian languages that provided a foundation for his illustrious career among American Indians, which lasted more than sixty years. Zeisberger's able assistant, John Heckewelder, of Moravian ancestry, also attained prominence as a missionary among the Indians. Besides his missionary labors, he was a postmaster, a justice of the peace, and a justice of the court of common pleas as well. In the last years of his life he engaged in literary pursuits which led to his election into the prestigious American Philosophical Society of Philadelphia. Thanks to Zeisberger's and Heckewelder's writings, we have accurate documentation of the life and customs of American Indians.

Another noteworthy personality among the Moravian Brethren was the organ builder David Tanneberger (1728-1804). Born of Moravian parents, on Count Zinzendorf's estate in Berthelsdorf, he was a skillful joiner, a notably good tenor, and an accomplished violinist. He learned the organ-building craft and soon became well-known for his unique technical skills. Organs of his manufacture were in high repute and were shipped all over eastern Pennsylvania from his Lititz shop, even to such distant places as Albany, New York.

The members of the Demuth family who came originally from Karlov, Moravia, were tobacconists by trade and successful merchants whose shop in Lancaster, Pennsylvania, still in existence, is the oldest of its kind in the entire United States. Some of their descendants were talented artists, particularly Charles Demuth, water-color illustrator and still-life painter, who is considered by some to be the predecessor of Andy Warhol.

Cultural contributions of Moravian Brethren from Czech lands were distinctly notable in the realm of music. The trumpets and horns used by the Moravians in Georgia are the first evidence of Moravian instrumental music in America. Johann Boehner

(1710-1785) from Zelená Hora, Moravia, is the first recorded Moravian instrumentalist. The program of music in Bethlehem, Pennsylvania, was greatly stimulated by the arrival in 1761 of two talented musicians, Jeremiah Dencke, a Silesian, and Immanuel Nitschmann, a Moravian. Johann Frederick Peter of Silesia is considered to be the first Moravian composer in America, having composed over eighty hymns. The America-born Christian Till, of Bohemian ancestry, who succeeded Peter as organist of the Bethlehem church, was also a composer of reputation.

A survey of the Bohemian and Moravian presence in Colonial America would not be complete without saying a few words about the descendants of the first known settlers from the Czech lands, i.e., Augustine Herman and Frederick Philipse. In one of my earlier essays,[12] I wrote that the finest legacy Augustine Herman left behind was his living legacy, represented by his progeny. Although his male line and name became extinct in 1739, Hermann's three daughters and the female issue of his grandson left numerous descendants "filling the annals of the worthy and the rich." Based on numerous genealogical and historical sources, this author has been able to identify a number of distinguished personalities—U.S. senators, congressmen, state governors, supreme court justices, members of presidents' cabinets, and other men and women of substance—who are linear descendants of Augustine Herman. The same holds true about the descendants of Herman's contemporary, Frederick Philipse. I should like to conclude with an old saying: *"Čech se ve světe neztratí"* (A Czech won't get lost in the world).

The Czech-American Journalist:
A Bridge Between the
Old Country and the New

Peter Bísek

I am the publisher of *Americké Listy*, an independent Czech and Slovak bi-weekly, printed in Glen Cove, just outside of New York. Our twelve page newspaper started in April 1990 under the name *Československý týdeník* (in English this means Czechoslovak Weekly), and this year we changed the name to the more appropriate *Americké Listy* (which could be loosely translated into "American Leaves"). We renamed our newspaper because the old name—*Czechoslovak Weekly*—did not reflect the reality: Czechoslovakia does not exist anymore and we never became weekly. Also, with that new name—*Americké Listy*—we picked up where our predecessors, Mr. Frank Švehla and his wife Gerda, left off in November 1989.

A very brief look at history is appropriate here. In 1911, Tomáš Čapek, in his book *Fifty Years of Czech Press in America*, listed 342 titles of Czech-American periodicals that had existed up to that year in the U.S. The list broke down into so many groups and subgroups that I could not even name them here for lack of time.

Just to illustrate: Čapek breaks down the heading "Political," into Republican, Democratic, Populist, Socialist, Anarchist, etc. And there are periodicals "popular with pictures," "popular without pictures," "humorous," or "written for youth." He also includes the headings Religious (mainly Catholic and Protestant), Anti-religious, and Atheistic. Under the heading Special, he lists medicine, health, sports, and physical fitness. Professional is subdivided into economic, entrepreneurial, and commercial. He also has societal, theatrical and literary headings, listing occasional and literary periodicals and women's almanacs. He even lists a title as "English but with a Czech soul."

Around the turn of the twentieth century there were eight Czech daily newspapers in the U.S., eight that came out twice a week, thirty-two weeklies, four bi-weeklies, twenty-two monthlies and four occasionals. Unbelievable, isn't it? Naturally, not all existed at the same time, but the numbers are shocking nevertheless. František Kořízek published the very first Czech newspaper in the United States, the weekly *Slowan Amerikánský* (American Slav) starting on January 1, 1860, in Racine, Wisconsin. Only three weeks later, on January 21, the famous weekly *Národní Noviny* was born in St. Louis, Missouri. Its editor-in-chief, Franta Mráček, kept them alive only for a year and a half. In October 1861 Mráček continued publishing, this time bi-weekly, *Slávie*, also in Racine.

And then came *Zvony*, *Pozor*, *Pokrok*, *Katolické Noviny*, *Bratrské Listy*, *Národní Noviny*, *Amerikán*, *Pokrok Západu*, *Hlas*, *Diblík*, *Bič*, *Hus*, *Rarášek*, *Chicagský Věstník*, *New Yorkský Deník*, *New Yorkské Listy*, and many more. Maybe you have heard of them? One Břetislav Sedlecký and "comrades" (*soudruzi* in Czech) published *Free Spirit* in 1895. Hugo Chotek managed to print just one issue of a weekly *By the Fireplace* in 1901. There were so many Czech printers around Chicago that they had their own union and free monthly *Typograf České Typografické Unie C. 330* (Typograph of the Czech Typographical Union Chapel 330 — Chapel stands for a local branch of the Typographical Union.)

What I am going to talk about now for a few minutes probably concerns only the first generation of Czech-Americans and, to a certain degree, their children. The third, fourth, and older generations of Czech-Americans, already full-blooded Americans for the most part, still speak various dialects of the Czech language. But very few can read Czech. The periodicals of their clubs, societies, and organizations are printed mostly in English and address the concerns and interests of their lives in the United States. As a naturalized first-generation American, it would be foolish of me to pretend that I can speak and write about their needs.

During the last forty years, most Czech-American newspapers published outside Czechoslovakia were involved in a bloodless, but brave war against the communist regime in the old country. The Velvet Revolution of 1989 brought a basic change in the purpose, and therefore in the content, of these newspapers. The establishment of a democratic system of government in the old country brought new responsibilities on the part of the publishers of the Czech newspapers and periodicals abroad.

The new regime in Czechoslovakia—finally in the form we had all fought for—needs to be helped, not fought against. But the transition from the state of confrontation between the old regime and the Czech-American newspapers to peaceful and friendly cooperation is not an easy one.

The euphoria that followed the fall of communism in 1989 was shared across the wide spectrum of Czech-Americans and Americans in general. It seemed that the proverbial bridge between the exiles and the old country which had been in ruins since 1948 would be quickly repaired. Soon it would be open to pedestrians from both sides.

But the euphoria did not last long enough for the bridge to be fixed. In a short time, perhaps in a matter of months, it became more and more difficult to explain to our readers where our beloved, reborn country was heading and why. How could one defend the fact that many of the former communists were in the new Czechoslovakian government? That the Communist Party of Czechoslovakia was declared evil by law but was not outlawed and put out of business? (Even today the Communist Party has the largest membership of all political parties in the Czech Republic.) This shows that there is a mental gap between Czech-Americans, who would outlaw the party, and Czechs, who have re-elected it in free elections.

It was, and still is, very difficult to satisfy our readers with true reporting from the old country. Many of the new laws—hastily written and rewritten by the new Czechoslovakia practically every day—seem to be aimed, at the very least, at ignoring the aspirations of our readers if they are not antithetical to their interests. Consequently, instead of a friendly dialogue, too much criticism went back and forth across the Atlantic. Even though this criticism was many times valid, it certainly did not improve the sensitive relationship between Czech exiles and the old country. The bridge that needed so much tender, loving care in repairing, developed even more cracks.

Then came the infamous division of the country in 1993. Again, Czech-Americans were not heard. They had no voice in the legislative process. As if old wounds were not painful enough, this lightning struck before they were healed, creating a new crisis when the old country broke into two new republics: the Czech Republic and Slovakia. Many exiles could not understand the reason for it; therefore, they would not accept it. The badly needed dialogue between Czechoslovaks there and here became even more limited. For many Czech-Americans it was nonexistent.

To make matters worse, the Czech legislators and the representatives of the new Czech government did not make a serious attempt to communicate with the exiles, did not reach out to them, nor even try to fulfill the promise of Václav Havel, the Czech president, who said in his 1990 New York visit, that Czechs living abroad are just one branch of a big Czech tree.

The exiles were not united, did not speak with one voice. That is true. Still, a friendly gesture was, and still is, expected today from the Czech government.

Our newspaper, *Americké Listy*, for one, is ready, willing, and eager to help both sides understand each other better, to embrace each other, and to cooperate. Being Czech-Americans, we first strive to represent the interests of our Czech-American readers. We strive to provide a forum for the Czech-American community. For example, in the latest issue of *Americké Listy* we have a condensed report on Czech pensions—or whatever is left of them—being paid to Czech-Americans. These pensions were vandalized by the new arbitrary ruling of the new Czechoslovak government.

This is one of the several pressing issues on the minds of Czech-Americans today, waiting to be addressed and resolved.

And the future? You might be surprised, but I am optimistic about the future of the Czech-American newspapers. Let me tell you why.

First of all, there are many new technologies—desk top publishing, fax, and the internet—opening new horizons and creating new opportunities in publishing. It is not less expensive to publish an ethnic newspaper today than ten years ago, but certainly it is easier.

Secondly, I firmly believe that the ethnic newspapers will never die in this great country. That goes for Czech and Slovak language newspapers as well. Even though our (American) immigration laws strictly limit the number of Europeans that can come here legally, I do not think that it will significantly diminish the need for Czech and Slovak language newspapers. Their shape and content might change from time to time, but they will be here 100 years from today. Hopefully, they will be even stronger.

This is because of the strength of the printed word and because of the bond that unites Czechs in the two countries. Sports arenas and stadiums did not disappear with the invention of television; the proliferation of movie rental stores did not close down movie houses. An average American watches TV more than ever but at the same time refuses to give up the pleasure of turning the pages and reading.

Far removed and mostly out of touch with their homeland, the Czech-Americans will always want to know what is going on in that old country. Television and movies will never be enough. Czech-Americans will want to read in the language of their mothers and fathers. And there will always be someone like us who will want to serve them.

Finally, I am optimistic about the future of the Czech-American newspapers because I sense a genuine desire on the part of new Czech representatives, namely Ambassador Alexandr Vondra and Consul General Petr Gandalovič, to work together with us Czech-Americans on solving the problems. And they are not alone. The chairman of a new Committee on Czechs Living Abroad of the Czech Congress, Mr. Milan Špaček, faxed me from Prague just this week a message which ends with this sentence: "We hope that this is the beginning of a fruitful cooperation between Czech expatriots and the Czech Republic. Let us all hope that a new beginning it is."

Americké Listy is certainly not the first Czech-American newspaper, and I firmly believe that it is not the last one either. As there were many before us, there will be many after we are gone.

We are just one link in a long chain. Links of this chain are sometimes strong, at other times weak and frayed, but together they reach back across 150 years of the history of the Czech-Americans and across the thousands of miles between our two countries.

In closing let me support my optimism about the future of Czech-American newspapers with a short story:

There was a gathering of Czech-Americans at the turn of the century attended by a father and a teenage son. Speeches were made, Czech dances were danced, and when Czech songs were sung, the father started to cry quietly. "What is the matter, Dad? What happened?" asked the son. "Well, my son," the father replied, "I am sad because my generation is the last one that speaks Czech, dances Czech dances, and sings Czech songs. You will not be doing it when you are my age. That's why I am sad." This happened three generations ago. And it will probably keep happening three generations in the future.

Genealogy:
Building a Bridge to the Past

Daniel Hrna

Webster's Dictionary defines genealogy as the tracing of one's descent. More than that it is an account or history of the descent of a person or family from a common ancestor. Technically it is the enumeration of ancestors and their descendants in the natural order of succession.

Webster's also defines a bridge as a passageway over an obstacle. Our obstacle is time, the great barrier between today and the past. In genealogy we build an invisible bridge to the past. Just as the builders of a more visible structure such as the Golden Gate Bridge of San Francisco required steel and cement, so we too need the material and tools to build our bridge to the past. We also need a foundation for our bridge. Genealogy has devised tools and materials that we can use to build our foundation and gateway through time.

When we speak of time travel, one of my favorite science fiction programs was called *Dr. Who*, a B.B.C. series aired on National Public Television a few years ago. Dr. Who was a "time lord" who had the equipment with which to travel through time and space. His vehicle was an English telephone booth called the Tauris. The imagination of writers cannot physically substitute the Tauris for our time travel. There is no magic! We have to use the tools available to us in the form and quality that currently exist, recognizing the damage done to many homes, churches, public buildings, cemeteries, and records lost and destroyed over the long period of history. Fortunately for us, many of these tools still endure, and supporting material is also available.

To begin the journey to find our ancestral history, and perhaps even know how these people lived so long ago, we begin at home. We look for family bibles, family histories, pictures with information on the back, letters carefully kept over the years, newspaper articles, death notices, marriage notices—every piece of minutiae that may be still available.

It is a fact that many of the immigrants from the Czech and Slovak lands worked hard to provide for their families. Many had difficulty with the English language. Many of the immigrants soon forgot to keep reminders of their homeland. Often the children discarded this information. Many children raised as Americans too soon lost the language and culture of their forefathers. Friends and relatives died, the information was lost forever. Soon we come to a blank wall and cannot go any further. This is the point where we begin to use our tools and any material we may have collected.

We know that our ancestors have been buried in this country. Our best option, when all other searches fail, is to visit the burial places. Quickly we can find the tombstone that has been erected by the family. Often times the marker is the first reference. It tells us the birth and death dates, and often the geographical origin of the family member. Many times we will find the village of origin listed on the cemetery marker. In my case, the village of origin was Halenkov, Moravia.

Since we know that a death occurred, many records are available to us in the United States. One source that can give us good information is the probate court records, that is, the legal records involving the last will and testament of the deceased. The probate record will give us a look at the will, the inventory, and other information on the heirs. The will gives the names of the spouse and children. The inventory will give us a list of assets. The deed records will give information about what property was purchased and sold by an ancestor. Most of our ancestors became U.S. Citizens. These records are recorded in local county courthouses and are easily accessible. Being good citizens, they participated in the census count every ten years. Some census records are very accurate: they give the names of all of the family members in the home; their birth data; and both dates and places of birth.

Another useful tool that we have is the research of Mr. Hejl and Mr. Baca, who have worked on obtaining the passenger records for the period of time when most Czech immigrants arrived. Although not always including extensive narration, the records are informative because they note the village of origin of the family members who came to America. Often, one will find several families with the same surname arriving within a short time of each other. Mr. Baca will address this issue in the following essay.

Birth and death records are obtained locally and sometimes at the state capitol. These records give the parentage and grandparents. The death records usually reflect the maiden names of the spouses. Marriage records are a good source for the maiden name of the ancestor. Local newspapers are good for feature articles about local people and often have very complete obituaries.

Armed with these tools and materials, we are ready to start on our quest for the holy grail of genealogy—our ancestral origins.

I will relate an anecdote to bring into perspective how genealogy works and how it produces fascinating results.

Recently I was visiting with my daughter in Crested Butte, Colorado. Crested Butte is basically a ranching and mining community. I had a few free hours one Sunday afternoon. Being a history buff, I love to visit old cemeteries to find out how people lived long ago. I have seen epitaphs on markers in New Mexico with notations such as these: "Died of Throat Troubles"—the deceased had been hanged! Very frequent are epitaphs stating that the deceased had died with the "Aid of a Doctor." The cemetery was small but old, dating back to the 1880s and maybe earlier. As I walked past the tombstones, I noticed that almost all of the epitaphs were written in a Slavic language. Very few English epitaphs were inscribed from the turn of the century. I noticed that it was not Czech but another language of the Slavonic group. It was easy to decipher the cognates as lives, deaths, wives, fathers, sons, daughters, and infants. It began to intrigue me that these were of

Slavic origin: but what group? One family name particularly stood out, with several members having the same surname. Especially intriguing was the information that a son, who was born in 1900, had died in 1923. Another marker was etched "Mother and Child, age 22." Obviously the young mother died in childbirth. Other family markers also had Slavic inscriptions. I finally found a marker that read, "Born in Yugoslavia." Excited with my find, I quickly looked for any markers with decedents from Slovenia or Croatia. I did find one very old tombstone with the phrase, "Born in Croatia." This led me to conclude that a large number of early settlers were from Croatia.

I went to town and learned from some of the natives that indeed this had been a Croatian settlement, with Italians being the other group of early settlers. This was a coal mining and ranching area. So it was natural for these people who did the same type of work in Europe to settle in this area. In fact, the current town hall used to be the old "Croatian Hall"! In Gunnison, I found a book entitled "History of Crested Butte." In this book of family histories, I found the name of the young man who died at the age of twenty-three in a single paragraph from a family history. He died while crossing the old Monarch Pass at 12,000 feet during the winter; his car apparently left the road, and he froze to death in the intense Colorado cold.

So the life and times of Crested Butte begin to come alive when we apply the genealogical tools at our disposal.

The land that this family owned was in litigation. The heirs had wanted to sell their large tract of land, but the deal fell through. This gave me a new lead to search. By going to the land records, I was able to trace the family ownership of the land; the probate records identified the heirs, and inventories gave the amount of land ownership. The tax records gave the tax sales and suggested how difficult life was in those early days. In fact I was able to trace the family and their land to the initial government land grant and mineral rights.

Not only can we build a bridge to the past, but we can glimpse into that past!

Documenting Czech Immigrant Arrivals

Leo Baca

Introduction

Invariably, Czech-American genealogists and family historians reach the point of asking how their ancestors came to America. Many questions come to mind. What was the name of the ship? When did they immigrate? How long was the voyage? What did the ship look like? What was the port of entry? In answering these questions, a significant amount of research needs to be done.

When Did They Immigrate?

While family tradition can tell you a great deal about your ancestor's immigration to America, you will want to see how much of the tradition can be supported by documentation. Even with little or no information, you can still proceed with the search. One of the first things you should do is to check the 1900, 1910, or 1920 censuses. If you can find and positively identify your ancestors in these censuses, you will have gained some important information because these censuses show the year of immigration to America. You will also know whether or not your ancestor was naturalized by the year 1900, 1910, or 1920. These censuses, of course, show all sorts of other data of interest to genealogists, such as month and year of birth, the number of years married, the number of children living, and so forth.

If the date of immigration is shown before 1880, then you need to check those intervening censuses. This will give you some idea of whether your ancestors moved around. Knowing where your ancestors lived at a particular time will give a clue as to where to look for naturalization records. Naturalization records are important because they give the name of the port of embarkation, when your ancestor left, and when and where he or she arrived in America. Before 1906, naturalization proceedings took place in district courthouses, which are located in the county seats. You may need to search several different district courthouses until you find your ancestor's naturalization record.

Some Czech immigrants did not bother with naturalization. Others were slow in doing so. I have one ancestor who came to this country in 1872 as a small child, but he was not naturalized until 1926. In his case, I found his naturalization papers with the Immigration and Naturalization Service (INS).

Passenger Lists

After you have identified the port and date of entry, you will want to see if you can find the passenger list for the ship on which your ancestor arrived. Knowing the particular port through which an ancestor entered the United States may limit the difficulty of your search.

Since the National Archives is the custodian of passenger lists, you should learn what is available. *The Guide to Genealogical Research in the National Archives* is an excellent place to start. You may also wish to peruse *Immigrant and Passenger Arrivals: A Select Catalog of National Archives Microfilm Publications*. Both are available from the National Archives Trust Fund Board, Washington, D.C. 20408.

There are two kinds of passenger lists. They are the customs passenger lists and the immigration passenger lists. Customs passenger lists were prepared by the captains of the ships bringing the immigrants to the United States. These lists were filed with the collectors of customs in compliance with an Act of Congress approved on March 2, 1819 (3 Stat. 489), and later acts. In later years, another kind of list was prepared. It is called an immigration passenger list.

The important thing to remember about passenger lists is the fact that the captain was required to turn in a list at each port of call in the United States. The customs passenger lists gave the passenger's name, age, occupation, and country of origin. The heading gave the date and port of departure as well as the embarkation port and date.

The immigration authorities at the port of entry recopied these passenger lists turned in by the captain of the ship onto a separate document called an "Abstract." The original passenger list was retained by the immigration authorities at this port of call. The "Abstract" was sent to Washington, D.C. Both the "custom passenger list" and the "abstracts" were, in later years, placed in the National Archives, Washington, D.C. for safe keeping. Microfilm copies of those passenger lists and abstracts can be purchased from the National Archives. In addition, microfilm copies can be rented from a number of sources.

If your ancestor arrived at the port of Baltimore, you are in luck. Passenger lists are available for the years 1820-1952. Best news of all, the passenger lists are indexed. There are a number of Soundex indices for this time period. The data available for immigrants who arrived in New Orleans is also good. Customs passenger lists are available for the years 1820 to 1902. There is also an index available: T527, 1853-1899. Immigration passenger lists are available from January 1903 to 1952. There is an index (T618, available for 1900-1952 arrivals).

Good data is also available for the port of New York. Customs passenger lists cover the years 1820-1897. There is an index (M261) for the years 1820-1846, and there is an index (T519) that begins on June 16, 1897 and ends on June 30, 1902. In addition, there is a Soundex index (T621) for arrivals between July 1, 1902 and December 31, 1943. Immigration passenger lists show the town that the immigrant left, and where he or she was going in the United States. So if one of your ancestors immigrated in the 1890s or later, you will have some interesting research possibilities.

Up to now, only passenger lists in America have been discussed. However, there were passenger lists that were left with European authorities. The most famous of these are the Hamburg passenger lists. They are available at the Library of Congress and at branch genealogical libraries of the Church of Jesus Christ of Latter Day Saints (sometimes called Mormons).

If your ancestors emigrated through Bremen, there are a limited number of problems because the Bremen passenger lists were destroyed. Even with that, there are still some possibilities. Copies of some passenger lists were published in the *Deutsche Auswanderer-Zeitung*. If you wish to pursue this further, you can write to: Staatsarchiv Bremen, President-Kennedy Platz 2, 2800 Bremen 1, Germany. Some Bremen passenger lists were also published in the *Allgemeine Auswanderer-Zeitung* even though it was printed in Hamburg.

In the United States, several newspapers published passenger lists that included Czech arrivals. In Texas these include the Galveston *Die Union*, the *Neu-Braunfelse-Zeitung*, and the Galveston *Daily News*. The Nebraska *Pokrok Západu* carried passenger lists in 1879, and the Wisconsin *Slavie* also published passenger lists on occasion.

What About the Ship?

If you are interested in learning about the physical details of your immigrant ancestor's ship, the best overall source is Lloyd's *Universal Register*. The Library of Congress has a copy of one of these that was published in 1886. This was a grand attempt at cataloging all the world's ships over 100 tons. It divided the ships into two categories: sailing vessels and steamships. The *Universal Register* listed the name of the ship, the material that the vessel was made of, what kind of vessel it was (bark, brig, and so forth), what flag the vessel flew, the port of registry, net tonnage, the vessel's dimensions, the circumstances of its construction, and finally, who the owners or managers were. As a note of caution, Lloyd's has published registers of ships that it insures since the early 1800s, but the *Universal Register* is totally different because it also includes ships not insured by Lloyd's.

Other good sources are *Passenger Ships of the World Past and Present* by Eugene W. Smith and *Ships of our Ancestors* by Michael J. Anuta.

If you are interested in pictures of your immigrant ancestor's ship, you could search naval museums around the world. However, there is a fair chance you might find a picture of the ship you are looking for at either of the following:

Steamship Historical Society of America, Inc.
University of Baltimore Library
1420 Maryland Avenue
Baltimore, Maryland 21201-5782

Peabody Museum
East India Square
Salem, Massachusetts 01970

Publications

To date, six books entitled *Czech Immigration Passenger Lists*, Volumes I-VI have been published. Volume I lists Czech arrivals in Galveston between 1848 and 1871, as well as Czech arrivals in New Orleans between 1852 and 1879. There is also a section on Czech arrivals in Baltimore and New York in 1879 based on accounts published in the Nebraska Czech newspaper *Pokrok Západu*. Volume II contains the names of Czech arrivals in New Orleans between late 1879 and 1899 and Czech arrivals in Galveston between 1896 and 1906. Volume III was restricted to Czech arrivals in Galveston between 1906 and 1914. Volume IV deals with Czech arrivals in New York between 1847 and 1869. Volume V lists Czech arrivals in New York between 1870-1880. Volume VI contains Czech arrivals in New York, 1881-1886, and in Galveston, 1880-1886. These books contain the names of 104,910 Czech immigrants. Anyone wishing to obtain copies of these publications should write to me for information concerning price and availability. My address is: 1707 Woodcreek, Richardson, Texas 75082-4524.

Current Research

I am currently completing an abstract of Czech arrivals in New York during 1893. This will become part of Volume VII which will cover Czech arrivals in New York between 1887 and at least 1893.

The Moravian Folk Song:
The Best Means of Preserving
Czech Culture in Texas

Joseph N. Roštinský

Not all peoples possess great epic narratives extolling heroic virtues. Yet, all of them seem to have folk songs: simple or intricate tunes, composed as a rule anonymously in order to enforce the rhythm of the lyrics upon the mind of a nation. The folk song thus functions as a treasure-trove of historical memory. It transposes, as it were, an unknown individual's experiences onto the level of general application. That is why the folk song tends to address especially personal qualities and varied states of mind.

The folk song is one of the most essential "old ways," as it never anticipates the events to come; the future, as it were. It seems to be in the nature of the folk song that it merely summarizes the past, thus leaving the present open not only to the influence of the bygone times and frequent nostalgia, but also to its didactive appeal.

Nevertheless, the essentially temporal flow of events, as described in the lyrics, is predominantly oriented towards the present. The folk song teaches and admonishes through an example. Among all the artistic genres, produced anonymously, it may be paradoxically the least metaphoric one. It refers to its subject matter in a causal way, though it occasionally conceals intentional motives in the form of natural topoi. Inanimate and animate

44

objects (animals, birds, flowers, trees, rivers, etc.) are addressed as if they could actively participate in episodic acts of human drama. They are charged with a rather conventional symbolic message which is instantaneously understood both by the performer and the listener, provided they share the same cultural codes. In other words, the meaning of the folk song is far less obscure than that of many a poem. It is the primary function of the folk song to facilitate the process of communication through the creation of an idiomatic language typifying a particular ethnic group.

For the Texas-Czech community, the above generalizations translate into a series of practical instances of preserving the Czech folk song in an ethnic enclave. Specifically, the vast majority of the Texas Czechs does not belong to the Czech nation proper, that is to say, to the Bohemian branch of the contemporary Czech nation, but are of Moravian ancestry. The historical Czech population of Texas was indeed mainly Moravian. In the second half of the nineteenth century, the Moravians constituted an independent ethnic group that was rather remote from the Bohemian Czechs when it came to national consciousness. Hence there was occasional political friction between the Bohemian and Moravian political representatives and the substantially different cultural development of the two Czech lands.

Even today, Bohemia and Moravia are two distinct ethnographic regions despite the pervasive influence of contemporary mass culture, which have preserved their mutually opposed characteristic features. Although Moravia has been often described as a transitional ethnic territory, there is no doubt that it is a politically cognizable historical region which has developed its own idiosyncratic language of cultural discourse. Put in plain terms, it simply means that the Moravians know that they are Moravians, although they may communicate in a variety of dialects of the codified Czech vernacular. It would then appear as falsely overzealous to fit the historical concept of the Moravian into the straitjacket of the Czech, equaled Bohemian, national consciousness. It is by no means an exercise of nationalistic proportions when the Texas Moravians have traditionally claimed to be Moravians as distinct from the Bohemians. They would have hardly referred to themselves as Czechs, since that was a designation of the later vintage.

Why should all this actually matter? Indeed, it should, provided we wish to see the truly historical context within which the Texas Moravians and also some Bohemians had to culturally function in the initial stage of their colonization of Texas. The more descriptive ethnic background also helps us to better understand the remnant idiolects, as they have by now survived in individual families and sporadic communities. It would be equally interesting to contemplate a rather spontaneous distribution of the dominant Czech-Bohemian mass culture in the form of popular music which has exercised such a mighty influence on the Texas Moravian culture. The very fact that the Bohemians who settled in the North of the United States were far better organized in various fraternal associations (thanks mainly to their closer socioeconomic ties with the German Americans) and could express their views in the Czech language newspapers and journals is significant for the understanding of the vector of cultural influence upon the Texas Moravians.

It has been time and again documented that most of the Moravians and Bohemians arriving in Texas had been only minimally prepared to communicate in English, the reason being that the English language at the turn of the nineteenth century was sporadically taught in Central Europe. The aristocratic and educated classes learned German and French, the two languages considered to be paramount in the age of cultural refinement. Whoever wished to study English would have been looked upon as an adventurous student of the overtly practical and pragmatic Anglo-American civilization for which the "better" classes of the aristocratic Central Europe had very little understanding. In other words, the Moravian and Bohemian immigrants would have had almost no chance of studying English in their home country. They could, as a rule, comprehend German, up to a certain degree.

The language problem seems to have been the primary reason for the initial wave of Moravian and Bohemian newcomers to Texas to settle in linguistically homogeneous areas, be they Czech or German. The linguistic diversification in an ethnic group notwithstanding, the cultural affinities would become overwhelmingly determinant. In the concrete terms of folk music this cultural affinity means the pervasive influence of the Biedermeier style in popular music. It lingered in the Czech popular culture well into the second half of the nineteenth century. This was also the common denominator of the Moravian and Bohemian, as well as the Czech and German, cultural affinities. The brass band—far from being truly "native" to Moravia—became the codified ethnic symbol of the cultural difference. The waltz and polka would thus function as the dominant rhythms in the musical vocabulary of the Texas Moravians and Bohemians.

What then happened to the real Moravian folk song? Why is it that it has been almost obliterated and replaced by the more popular polka band tune? The extant research, conducted by the students of the things Czech in Texas, indicates that the Moravian folk song could not survive in its "pristine" form (provided there ever was any) within the close proximity of the popular Czech culture. Because it was, above all, the popular culture which found its way to Czech parish schools and church choirs. As a result, the Moravian folk song was inevitably marginalized as an esoteric musical genre incomprehensible to the following generations of the Texas Czechs.

The first encounter with the Texas Czech popular culture can leave only indelible memories. So it was in my case when I came to Austin in 1975 to assume a temporary teaching position of the Czech language at the University of Texas. It became gradually apparent to me that the Czech ethnic music, as interpreted by several Texas polka bands, was the decisive communication medium of the Texas Czechs and in particular of my U.T. students. They were not only enthusiastic dancers, but also wonderful singers. Shortly after my arrival at the university, I organized a singing group whose members were mostly students of the Czech language. They began to call themselves the University Czech Singers. Despite the differences in their major fields of academic interest, they had one common hobby: to learn and perform Czech folk songs. It was at this time that I decided to reintroduce the Moravian folk song to the Texas Czech musical heritage.

In 1977 the University Czech Singers produced their first and only LP stereo record entitled *Czechoslovakian Folksongs* (Houston, Doggett Independent Prod.). In the Texas Czech community, the record became an instant hit and was sold out in no time. One might say, it has become a collector's item by now. The people who made this happen deserve to be mentioned here. They are Beverly Gavenda, Robert Ermis, Sheri Prasatik, Dolores Eicher, Mary Ann Hlavac, Dennis Vacula, Marilyn Vacula, Dennis Kubiak, Helen Kubiak, Dennis Jasek, Joseph Ehrenberger, Roger Kolar, Gail Kana, Alex Chamberlain, Bobby Horton, Georgia Chamberlain, Woody Smith, and J. C. Ermis. There were other occasional participants in the singing performances, among whom I wish to mention Clinton Machann and James Holmes.

During their existence the University Czech Singers traveled to several Texas-Czech communities to perform at various folk festivals, meetings, Westfest, Austin's Aquafest, and even at the Taylor Nursing Home. The Moravian folk song was beginning to penetrate the polka band repertoire. It got into the song books of other Texas Czech singers. In 1985 the Dallas Czech Singers included some of the Moravian folk songs into their *Pisnicky české. Czech Folk Song Collection* (Kingwood, Texas, Kay Graphics). The old Moravian folk tunes were rediscovered, so to speak.

Regardless of its potential benefit to the Texas-Czech reader, the Dallas Czech Singers' publication has one serious drawback: it lacks the music notation, which makes it less practical in the way of serving as a model. The text without music hardly makes the song audible. For studying purposes, however, the publication has its own merits, as it shows in what way and to what extent the original text of the folk song has undergone a change in meaning. A case in point is the Moravian folk song *Okolo měsíca*. The University Czech Singers performed the song in the Moravian Slovak dialect (southeast Moravian region, called Moravské Slovacko). The protagonists of the text are the penniless Moravian young men who are trying to get money in order to buy for themselves new trousers (highly decorated and thus expensive folk costume). The Dallas Czech Singers' version is diametrically opposite. It is the young Czech women who are looking for "thousands," because they own nothing but their single dress which they wash on Friday, starch on Saturday, and on Sunday put on to show off on the street. Needless to say, the two versions of the same song express an entirely different folk sentiment. Moreover, the Dallas version is written in the literary Czech language.

The comparison of the two texts could lead to a further

analysis and various interpretations. Indeed, this might become fertile ground for academic research and a new exegesis of the structural components of the Moravian and Bohemian folk songs, as preserved in Texas. It may also lead to the discovery of the focal point where the revival of the Moravian folk song occurred twenty years ago. It goes without saying that the revival of the Moravian culture in Texas could not have been accomplished without the cooperative effort of all the parties concerned. The generous support of SPJST, KJZT, and CESAT, and the enthusiastic participation of Texans (not only ones of Czech ancestry) in the activities of the University Czech Singers made the success story all the more possible.

What then is the moral lesson one can learn from this unique historical event when a handful of ardent university students and teachers embark on the project of performing Czech folk songs for the local community? In 1995 the University Czech Singers celebrated their twentieth anniversary at the First Reunion at Taylor, Texas. The choice of the place was determined by the fact that a former professor of Czech language and literature, Dr. Svatava Pirková Jakobson, had chosen the Taylor Nursing Home as her last address. We all felt that it was most appropriate to perform especially for her, as she was instrumental in the process of propagating and thus preserving the Texas-Czech heritage. Although she was born in South Bohemia, her heart beat was that of the Moravian folk music. Intuitively she recognized the potential wealth of folklore material scattered all over the Texas-Czech community. She traveled incessantly through the Texas-Moravian countryside, searching for new items for her extensive collection of Texas-Czech folklore, deposited now at the University of Texas at Austin. It is now up to future students of Czech studies in Texas to rediscover in the archives of the library their valuable cultural heritage which endows each individual human being with personal identity and existential meaning.

The Czech Heritage Society of Texas and Bridges to the Czech Republic

Robert Janak

Background

The Czech Heritage Society (CHS) of Texas is a young organization. It was founded in the fall of 1982 in Taylor, Texas. Although there are members in other states, and a few in the Czech Republic, most CHS members are Texans. Although the scope of the society is largely geared to Texas Czechs, there is a great interest in the Texas-Czech community in the history, culture and current events of their ancestral homeland.

From the Society's inception, many CHS members were engaged in some sort of contact with Czechoslovakia, which at that time was under Communist rule. Many breached the Iron Curtain as tourists, wanting to see, perhaps, the land of their ancestors. Others traveled to Prague as students and participated in the summer language programs sponsored by Texas A&M University and the University of Texas. Others visited relatives who were still living in the Old Country, or sought out information on their families in the state archives, or in their ancestral villages.

Combined with the activities of Czechs from other states, the travels of tourists from other countries, and the visits of artists and musicians in cultural exchange programs, these contacts constituted a constant influx of Westerners who helped keep the Czech population from cultural malnutrition in a Soviet-dominated colonial system and reminded them that they were people of the West and not people of the East. What is more, every rustle of the Iron Curtain fanned the not quite cold embers of freedom that lay hidden under layers of obeisance to the Soviet mentors.

With the triumph of the Velvet Revolution, and the abandonment of restrictive Communist policies, organizations based in the West were able to establish contacts in Czechoslovakia, and then the Czech Republic, outside the narrow bounds previously allowed. Such contacts proliferated, and, one by one, bridges were built across a chasm that had separated the Czech people from the West for four decades. These bridges not only allowed for two-way traffic between the Czech lands and their natural, traditional friends in the West, but they helped anchor the country firmly in the world of Western Civilization where it belonged.

The Czech Heritage Society played a part in this movement as well, albeit a relatively modest one. Its members received visiting groups from Czechoslovakia and the Czech Republic and sent delegations of their own to tour and perform. They established a studies program that would allow them to learn about their old-world culture and bring it back to Texas to disseminate in the local Czech community. They brought to Texas a bit of the Old Country in the form of a typical Wallachian belfry. They published information on emigration from nineteenth-century Moravia, which had been compiled by a Czech scholar.

Some of this activity was an extension of contacts made by CHS members before the Velvet Revolution. Some of it was the result of the vision and activities of CHS Trustee Victor Peter. Modest though these efforts may have been, combined with the activities of other such organizations, they helped ease the process by which the Czech people reclaimed their rightful place in the Western family of nations, and they made our lives much, much richer.

Polajka

Over the past few years CHS members have stepped forward to offer lodging and entertainment to Czechs traveling with various delegations and ensembles. This has allowed the development of many close cross-Atlantic friendships, and it has brought Czech culture to the heart of the Texas Czech community.

In 1992 CHS Trustee Victor Peter invited the eighteen-member folk ensemble *Polajka* to Texas. The dancers, singers, and musicians were led by Dr. Jaroslav Štika, director of the Wallachian Open-Air Museum in Rožnov, and Dr. Václav Mikušek, assistant director. Members of the ensemble were entertainers, but they were historians first, and while they were in Texas they wanted to document and experience Texas-Czech culture and life style.

Polajka visited a dozen Texas towns from Pasadena to Dallas to Victoria, and countless communities in between. Victor Peter, CHS Trustee Linhart Steffek, and CHS member Clarence Pertl took the group from destination to destination in rented vans and private cars. Several county chapters of the Czech Heritage Society donated money to help the ensemble defray expenses while they were in Texas; many CHS members put one or two members up for the night so the travelers could see for themselves how members of the Texas-Czech community lived. As *Polajka* performed for audiences around the states, they in turn enjoyed the performances of local Texas-Czech bands and orchestras. They learned much from us, and we learned much from them.

The Czech Heritage Society county chapters planned memorable stays for *Polajaka*. They took them on tours of the oldest Czech communities, churches, and cemeteries in the state. They took them to the headquarters of other Texas-Czech organizations and arranged for meetings with their leaders. They took them to local events and arranged for special activities, such as church picnics, hay rides, visits to local farms and ranches, and a trip to sample the hospitality and brew of the Spoetzl Brewery in Shiner.

While *Polajka* was in Caldwell to perform at the annual Kolache Festival, Dr. Štika and Dr. Mikusek met with the CHS Executive Committee and the CHS Board of Trustees, where personal contacts were made that later developed into joint projects between the Czech Heritage Society and the Wallachian Open-Air Museum. As was stated before, they learned a lot from us and we learned a lot from them. And the desire for further cooperation between the Czech Heritage Society and the museum was firmly established.

Lidice Rose

At the Fall meeting of the Czech Heritage Society in 1992, Willa Mae Cervenka, a member from Waco, made the motion for the Society to donate a rose bush to the Garden of Friendship and Peace at Lidice, the Bohemian village that Hitler destroyed in 1942 in a fit of rage and revenge after the assassination of *Reich-sprotektor* Reinhard Heydrich in Prague. The motion carried, and the following summer a delegation of CHS Executive Committee members made the presentation.

In June of 1993 CHS Vice President Carolyn Meiners led a Texas-Czech music ensemble to Rožnov to perform at the international Moravian Folklore Festival and Compatriots Days. Many of the twenty Fayette Czech Singers and Dancers were Czech Heritage Society members. Other society members accompanied the group.

The Fayette Czech Singers and Dancers performed four times at the festival. They sang traditional Czech melodies, as well as popular Texas and country and western tunes. Besides participating at the festival, along with groups from other countries, they visited their individual ancestral villages and toured places of historic and cultural interest in both the Czech Republic and Slovakia.

Five CHS Executive Committee members, including Carolyn Meiners, made the trip. They took advantage of their presence in the Czech Republic to go to Lidice to donate the CHS rose. A yellow rose was chosen—to symbolize the famed yellow rose of Texas. They dedicated it to the memory of all the Texas Czechs who died in foreign wars. One of the Lidice survivors attended the dedication ceremony. Afterwards she told the group of the tragic events that had transpired there some half century before.

The Lidice Rose remains for the Czech Heritage Society a nostalgic link to a sad era of Czech history that they missed because of their ancestors' earlier emigration to a part of the world that was spared the experiences of Hitler's reign of evil.

Wallachian Studies Program

The Czech Heritage Society is an organization with an educational mission. In April of 1993 the CHS Board of Trustees approved plans for a Wallachian Studies Program. The idea was to send a cadre of members to the Czech Republic to learn about the culture of Wallachia, the region in northeastern Moravia that sent most of the Czech immigrants to Texas. On their return they would be able to share the information they learned with the rest of the Texas Czech community.

The Wallachian Studies Program was sponsored jointly by the Czech Heritage Society and the Wallachian Open-Air Museum in Rožnov. The Czech Heritage Society selected participants and arranged air transportation. The Wallachian Museum arranged land transportation and room and board, and coordinated the program in Rožnov.

CHS Trustee Victor Peter negotiated arrangements for the program while he was a docent at the Wallachian Museum that same year. The museum officials for their part were eager to teach Texas Czechs about the culture of their forebears. After all, education was a large part of their job description.

The Wallachian Studies Program was held twice, in the summer of 1994 and in the summer of 1995. Each program was three weeks in duration, which included time for participants to venture off on their own, perhaps to do genealogical research, perhaps to find the villages of their ancestors.

While in Rožnov the Wallachian Studies Program participants were exposed to several aspects of regional folk culture. Many of the activities of the program were hands-on experiences. The participants learned how to paint Easter eggs and decorate gingerbread cookies. They learned how to make pottery and carve wood. They had a chance to blow glass and experiment with traditional meals. They also learned some traditional dances and had the opportunity to brush up on their Czech. They participated in folklife festivals held on the museum grounds and took field trips to sites of historical and cultural interest, including Prague.

The Czech Heritage Society thus created in Texas a pool of knowledge about Wallachian, Moravian, and Czech culture. On their return the participants were able to share what they learned throughout the Texas-Czech community. They wrote newspaper articles. They presented programs at CHS meetings. They spoke to other groups, and even visited schools and taught our children about their ancestral culture. The colorful traditions of the corner of Europe that sent so many emigrants to Texas came alive as those who had been to Rožnov displayed the peasant crafts they brought back and showed how to paint Easter eggs and make sauerkraut soup.

The Wallachian Studies Program had the additional result of creating long lasting friendships, because most of the participants were housed in private homes. Some of what was lost during the previous forty years of isolation and suppression was regained.

The Wallachian Studies Program was not held in 1996 or 1997. Not enough people signed up to repeat the program. But the Czech Heritage Society and the Wallachian Museum both have hopes of repeating the program in some format in the future. It was too successful not to hold again. It was too memorable an experience not to make available to others.

Festival of American Folklife

The last weekend in June and first weekend in July of 1995 saw the heart of Washington D.C. throb with Czech music, dance, and culture. The occasion was the twenty-ninth annual Festival of American Folklife, and the place was the National Mall. Every year different countries are invited to participate in the festival, demonstrating their crafts and sharing their culture. In 1995 the Czech Republic was one of the countries invited to participate.

Some sixty-six craftsmen, musicians, dancers, and folk artists traveled from the Czech Republic to Washington D.C., where they sang, danced, and demonstrated such traditional crafts as painting Easter eggs and making corn husk dolls. The Czech delegation was led by Dr. Jaroslav Štika, director of the Wallachian Museum. The Czech Heritage Society had had several years' contact with Dr. Štika and the museum, so it was natural for the Czech Heritage Society to participate in the event in whatever way possible.

The Smithsonian Institution and government of the Czech Republic each put up some $300,000 to cover expenses for the Czechs' participation in the event. An additional $100,000 remained to be raised through private and corporate donations. Daniel Hrna, Houston attorney and CHS Legal Advisor, was designated coordinator for raising the additional funds. CHS Trustee Victor Peter remained in frequent contact with Dr. Štika as plans for the festival were being made.

CHS President Carolyn Meiners led a delegation of officers, trustees, and CHS members to Washington to participate in the festival activities. Although they were not there in any official capacity, they renewed friendships and solidified relationships made when they had traveled to the Czech Republic, and when they hosted Czech groups touring the United States. Also, the representatives of the Czech Heritage Society were there to receive a magnificent gift from the Wallachian Museum to people of Czech descent in Texas.

Bell and Belfry

The Czech contingent to the Festival of American Folklife brought with them to Washington a bell, which was cast especially for the occasion by Josef Tkadlec of Halenkov, Moravia. Accompanying the bell was a belfry, which was assembled on the National Mall.

The belfry was designed in a typical Wallachian style. It was thirty feet tall, included a ten-by-ten-foot chapel topped with a wooden shingle roof, and built around a tree trunk stripped of its bark. The trunk was forked at the top, and in the fork hung the Halenkov bell. Above the bell was a canopy, the underside of which was painted with the words "*Co srdce pojí, moře nerozdvojí,*" or "What the heart joins, the sea cannot divide." This inscription is a reference to the close feeling of kinship between the Czechs of Bohemia and Moravia and their compatriots on the other side of the ocean. With the fall of the Communist system, the words were especially significant because of the reestablishment of close and open ties between the two branches of the Czech nation—those who had stayed behind and those who were now Americans.

The Wallachian belfry stood on the National Mall for the duration of the folklife festival. It is said that CHS Trustee Victor Peter stood in front of the belfry for hours, explaining to every passerby the significance of the belfry, and the meaning of the words painted thereon.

At the end of the folklife festival the Wallachian Museum donated the bell and belfry to the Czech Heritage Society. Now came the problem: how to get them to Texas, and what to do with them once there.

The belfry was taken apart, and Eugene Labay, CHS Trustee, and Ladislav Zezula of the Bexar County Chapter rented a truck and drove it and the bell to Texas. For over a year the bell and belfry were stored on the Zezula ranch in South Texas, while the Czech Heritage Society sought to find a suitable location for them.

Dr. Štika of the Wallachian Museum had suggested several sites as a possible home for the bell and belfry. Among them was St. Mary's Catholic Church at Praha in Fayette County. The CHS Board of Trustees deemed that Praha was an appropriate site because there the bell and belfry would be seen by the most people.

CHS Board Chairman Marjorie Matula entered into negotiations with Rev. Edward Bartsch of the Praha church and Bishop David Fellhauer of the Victoria Diocese, and on August 23, 1996, an agreement was signed placing the bell and belfry temporarily on the grounds of the church at Praha.

On November 10, 1996, at the annual Veterans Day Ceremony at Praha, the bell and belfry were dedicated to the memory of Victor Peter, who had done so much to reunite the two halves of the Czech nation on either side of the Atlantic.

Strnadel Book

In 1996 the Czech Heritage Society published *Emigration to Texas from the Místek District between 1856 and 1900*. The 207-page book contains extensive genealogical materials and valuable background information on nearly 3,000 Czech immigrants from northeastern Moravia to Texas. Both lists of vital statistics and translations of original documents supplement the historical text.

Drahomír Strnadel, who is currently the Mayor of Trojanovice, Moravia, began research for the book early in the 1980s. At that time he was in contact with Albert Blaha, a retired architect in Houston and founder of the Czech Heritage Society. Blaha was interested in immigration information from northeastern Moravia, because some eighty percent of the Czechs that came to Texas hailed from that region. Blaha and Strnadel could not exchange information openly because of restrictions imposed by the then Communist government of Czechoslovakia.

In 1989 Drahomír Strnadel traveled to Texas with a film crew to make a documentary on the Texas-Czech community. He brought along his research material in manuscript form which he planned to turn over to Albert Blaha. Unfortunately, on arrival in Texas he learned of Blaha's death. Strnadel then had to decide what to do with the research he had risked his career and well-being to undertake. He gave it to the Czech Heritage Society to publish and make available to the Czech people of Texas. Strnadel appointed three Texas-Czech scholars, all Czech Heritage Society members, to oversee the book's publication. They were Dr. Clinton Machann, Professor of English at Texas A&M University, Leo Baca, Texas-Czech historian and author in Richardson, and Robert Janak, CHS Trustee and foreign language teacher in Beaumont. Meanwhile, some of Strnadel's Texas friends donated $1,400 towards the book's publication.

The first task was to get the book translated into English. Mae Kainer, CHS Trustee and Houston travel agent, arranged for Alena Faltýsek of Prague to undertake the translation. The translated manuscript was returned to Texas, reviewed by the oversight committee and turned over to Marjorie Matula, Chairman of the Board of Trustees of the Czech Heritage Society to undertake its publication under the auspices of the CHS Victoria County Chapter.

Charles Spurlin, Professor of History at Victoria College in Victoria, volunteered the services of his secretary Sandy Summers to type necessary parts of the book as time allowed. The only thing that Prof. Spurlin asked for was one copy to be placed in the college library. Thus with donations and volunteered time and services from both within and outside the Texas Czech community, the book was completed.

Still, additional funds were needed to start the presses rolling. At the June 15, 1996, CHS Executive Committee meeting, eight CHS members pledged to lend the Czech Heritage Society $500 each for that purpose.

The CHS Board of Trustees originally planned to print 200

copies of the book. When advance orders started coming in, however, that figure was raised and raised again until it was decided to print 1,000 copies.

In the Fall of 1996 the book's author, Drahomír Strnadel, brought a delegation of fourteen businessmen from the Czech Republic to Texas. Strnadel, along with his group, was invited to attend the Fall meeting of the Czech Heritage Society in the Austin County community of Frydek. Members in attendance gave Drahomír Strnadel a standing ovation as CHS President Anna Krpec presented him with the fifth annual Texas Czech Heritage Award, an honor bestowed on individuals who have done a great deal to promote and preserve Czech heritage in the state. Strnadel graciously volunteered to autograph copies of his book, so it has become not only a valuable family history research tool, but a treasured family keepsake for many Texas Czechs.

Uncle Victor

Victor Peter was a retired businessman and CHS trustee. In 1986 and 1987 he served as the Society's vice president. He took as his charge the organizing of new county chapters, and during those two years the Czech Heritage Society enjoyed its most monumental growth, thanks largely to Victor Peter's indefatigable drive and gentle persuasion.

Following the Velvet Revolution, Victor Peter quickly established close ties with people in northeast Moravia, especially with the staff of the Wallachian Open-Air Museum in Rořnov. He acted as an intermediary between the Czech Heritage Society and the Czech community of Texas on one hand, and the Wallachian Museum and other Moravian authorities and personalities on the other.

In 1993 Victor Peter was invited by the Wallachian Museum to spend five months as a museum docent. He lived on the museum grounds in one of the peasant cottages on display and took foreign tourists on tours of the museum. He kept the Czech population of Texas apprised of the history and culture of Moravian Wallachia through his regular newspaper articles that appeared in the Czech-oriented publications in Texas. He also provided the people of Moravia with information on Texas-Czech culture and history, and on the lives of the descendants of the Czech emigrants that left their native Moravia so many years ago.

Victor Peter's frank and honest charm, his boundless good spirits, and his excellent command of antiquated Czech brought to Texas by his ancestors over a century before, ingratiated him with the local populace. In Moravia he was fondly known as Uncle Victor. Many of us in the Czech Heritage Society thought of him as Czech Texas' own ambassador to Moravia.

Victor Peter did more than anyone else in the Czech Heritage Society, and as much as anyone else in Czech Texas, to reestablish the close ties that once existed between the Czech people in the Old Country and their emigrant cousins, children, and grandchildren. He organized tours of the Czech Republic and orchestrated visits of Czech groups and delegations to Texas. He made the Czechs in the Old Country aware of the history and culture of the Texas Czech community, and he taught us about the lives and culture of our ancestors in their native Moravian villages. He negotiated joint projects between the Czech Heritage Society and the Wallachian Museum, and he was instrumental in bringing a bit of Moravia to Texas in the form of a specially cast bell and authentic Wallachian belfry.

Unfortunately Victor Peter fell victim to a cruel, debilitating disease that confined him to a hospital bed for a number of months. Always dedicated to his Czech heritage and to the many Czech-oriented organizations to which he belonged, he kept up contact by phone and through the visits of his many friends. Always the optimist, he proudly described each inch of his apparent recovery, which undoubtedly put him that much closer to his return to the Czech Republic with one group or another. But it was not to be.

Victor Peter's death in 1996 was profoundly felt on both sides of the Atlantic, and he was eulogized in both Czech and English. Uncle Victor, our own ambassador to the homeland of our ancestors, was the architect and builder of bridges that spanned both space and time, because they not only put us in contact with the Czechs of the present-day Republic, but they provided us with a route to a better understanding of our cultural and historic past.

Conclusion

These are some of the activities in which the Czech Heritage Society of Texas has engaged since the Velvet Revolution. They have not been earth-shaking. They have not been monumental. What they have been is part of a phenomenon that has resurfaced in the course of Czech history. That is the existence of close ties between the Czech people in the Old Country and their distant cousins, the descendants of emigrants who sought a better life abroad in the last century. Those ties became rather tenuous during the forty years of rule by a Communist government that glorified a common destiny with the Slavic colossus to the East.

Following the fall of Communism, however, old connections were quickly repaired and new bridges were built as Czech-American organizations reestablished the natural ties that bound them to the homeland of their ancestors. The Czech Heritage Society is proud and honored to have played whatever small role we have had in that historical process. And we are gratified by the enrichment it has brought to our own lives.

A Short History of the Czech Educational Foundation of Texas and Description of Its Current Projects

Clinton Machann

When the Czech Educational Foundation of Texas (CEFT) received its state charter as a non-profit organization on October 19, 1954, it was composed of three men who together served as its first board of directors: Henry R. Maresh, M.D., of Houston; Dr. John M. Skrivanek of College Station; and August Kacir of Temple. As stated in the charter, the purpose was to promote the Czech language and culture in Texas by supporting

> any educational undertaking by providing for, or making contri-
> butions as gifts or donations in cash or property to persons, or
> institutions engaged in the promotion of learning and under-
> standing of the Czech language and culture, the study of the ori-
> gin, structure, and modification of the Czech language and its
> grammatical relationships as given and preserved in literary
> embodiments, [and] the dissemination of information to the
> public concerning the importance of a knowledge of Czech and
> other Slavonic languages in our citizenry to the effective leader-
> ship of the United States of America in international affairs.

CEFT carried on the tradition of strong support for Czech language and culture in the state that had led to the establishment of the Department of Slavonic (later, Slavic) Languages at the

The SPJST lodge hall at Fayetteville, the first official lodge of that organization, which began operation in 1897.
— Photograph courtesy of Roger Kolar, with permission of the SPJST

The first ("Bila Hora") lodge hall at Ennis.
This lodge (SPJST #25) was founded in 1897.
— Photograph courtesy of Roger Kolar, with permission of the SPJST

The second lodge hall for Ennis' SPJST Lodge #25, built in 1923.
— Photograph courtesy of Roger Kolar, with permission of the SPJST

The "Praha" lodge hall at Taylor (SPJST Lodge #29) on its dedication day, July 1, 1934.
— Photograph courtesy of Roger Kolar, with permission of the SPJST

The "Komensky" lodge hall at Granger (SPJST Lodge #20) on its dedication day, August 9, 1909.

—Photo by Jno. P. Trlica

Pictured, from the left, are Howard Leshikar, SPJST president; Alexandr Vondra, ambassador of the Czech Republic; and Miloslav Rechcígl, SVU president, at a reception on the eve of the SPJST centennial celebration in July 1997.

—Photograph courtesy of *Věstník* and the SPJST

Pictured, from the left, are SPJST Legal Advisor Sidney Kacir, SPJST Vice-President Leonared Mikeska, and Helen and Albert Kubala (Members of SPJST Lodge #92, Fort Worth), at the SPJST centennial celebration in Belton, Texas.

— Photograph courtesy of *Věstník* and the SPJST

Pictured at the SPJST centennial celebration, from the left, are Meribeth Novak of SPJST Lodge #84, Dallas; Alexandr Vondra, ambassador of the Czech Republic; and Jason Hermis, of SPJST Lodge #142, Houston. Novak was chosen Miss SPJST and Hermis Mr. SPJST at the 1996 Convention in Arlington, Texas.

—Photograph courtesy of Věstník and the SPJST

Attendees at the SPJST centennial celebration examine copies of the SPJST 100th Anniversary Cookbook. More than 15,000 copies were sold, helping to fund various SPJST youth activities and a regional charity.

—Photograph courtesy of *Věstník* and the SPJST

Harry Czarnek performs with his band, the Texas Dutchmen, at the SPJST centennial celebration. Other musical groups featured during the two-day event included Jerry Haisler and the Melody Five, the Charles Mikeska Band, Brave Combo, Vrazels' Polka Band, and the Vanek Brothers of Victoria.

—Photograph courtesy of *Věstník* and the SPJST

Backstage at the SPJST centennial celebration, members of the choral group from SPJST Lodge #88 in Houston meet with Texas State Comptroller John Sharp, a member of SPJST Lodge #97 in Placedo. Organized in 1935 by Frank Hlavaty, the choral group currently performs at festivals throughout Texas and the southern United States. Other Czech-American performing groups at Belton included the Seaton Beseda Dancers from Lodge #47, the Dallas Czech Dancers from Lodge #130, and the West Dancers.

—Photograph courtesy of *Věstník* and the SPJST

Václav Havel, president of the Czech Republic and honorary member of SVU.

The Preservation of Czech-American Cultural Heritage
A Proclamation

On July 12 and I3, 1997, a conference entitled "Czech-Americans in Transition: Challenges and Opportunities for the Future" was held by the Czechoslovak Society of Arts and Sciences (SVU) in conjunction with the historic celebration of the 100th anniversary of the Slavonic Benevolent Order of the State of Texas (SPJST) in Belton, Texas

At this conference, educators, historians. social scientists, librarians, and other scholars joined with business people and community leaders to discuss key issues facing Czech-Americans and Slovak-Americans today: the preservation of language, folklore and folk art; ethnic history and genealogy; fraternal and cultural activities; the establishment and maintenance of archives, libraries, and cultural centers. An entire day was reserved for discussions of relations between the United States and the Czech Republic

United in a commonality of purpose, the undersigned believe that this historic event will mark the beginning of a warm friendship and mutually beneficial cooperation between the SPJST and SVU. Like other citizens of the United States and Canada, nations which thrive on cultural and racial diversity, the members of our organizations realize that there is no conflict between our loyalty to and love for the country where we live and our desire to preserve the rich and distinctive cultural heritage of our ethnic origins. We are also hopeful that activities such as the conference in Belton will enhance the social, cultural, political, and commercial relations between North America and Central Europe.

In this spirit, we will do our best to preserve the Czech, as well as the Slovak, cultural heritage in North America, and we call on all interested men and women to help us in this endeavor - particularly in efforts to encourage our children to learn about their heritage and to establish and promote cultural and language programs at universities throughout the United States and Canada, as well as educational exchanges with the Czech Republic and Slovakia.

Following the Velvet Revolution of November 1989, the members of many Czech and Slovak organizations in the United States and other Western countries felt that their work was done, but this feeling was premature. Our work has only begun, and cooperation among our various organizations is essential. We propose to establish a Cultural Heritage Commission, which would initially consist of representatives from the SVU and SPJST and later incorporate representatives of other major Czech and Slovak organizations in North America.

Miloslav Rechcigl, Jr.
President, SVU

Howard Leshikar
President, SPJST

Proclamation jointly signed by SVU President Rechcígl and SPJST President Leshikar shortly after the Belton conference.

Thomas Čapek, date unknown, probably in his office at Riverside Drive, Manhattan.

Thomas Čapek and his wife Anna, née Vostrovská, date unknown.
—Photograph courtesy of his granddaughter, Ludmila Leong

Thomas Čapek and his son, Thomas, Jr., date unknown, possibly in Záklasnák's photographic studio, New York.
—Photograph courtesy of the senior Čapek's granddaughter, Ludmila Leong

University of Texas. Many of the Texas Czechs who became active in CEFT had been members of *Čechie*, the Czech Club at UT-Austin. Among this group was Dr. John M. Skrivanek, who wrote a master's thesis at UT in 1946 entitled "The Education of the Czechs in Texas," before going on to study at Charles University in Prague, Czechoslovakia. One of the founders of CEFT, Dr. Skrivanek was a professor of Slavic languages who developed a Czech language program at Texas A&M University. Skrivanek long served as secretary-treasurer of CEFT, along with J. M. Skrabanek as president and the Rev. Joseph A. Barton as vice-president. Czech-Americans from across the state served on the board of directors during the early years. In addition to the founders and the officers mentioned above, the list includes R. J. Bartosh of Taylor, F. K. Bucek of Hallettsville, Charles Holasek of Corpus Christi, Joseph F. Holasek of West, Jaroslav Kleprlik of San Antonio, Tim Kostom of Houston, Vladimir Malec of Hallettsville, Edward L. Marek of Temple, Mrs. Henry R. Maresh of Houston, Joseph V. Maresh of Granger, Rev. A. W. Nesvadba of Wallis, I. C. Parma of Granger, Mrs. Benita Pavlu of Granger, E. W. Plasek of West, Cyril Pokladnik of Dallas, Ben Prevratil of Dallas, E. W. Schovajsa of Temple, Dr. John J. Shiller of Rowena, Joseph J. Skrivanek of Caldwell, Rudy Sefcik of West, Senator L. J. Sulak of La Grange, and Stephen Valcik of Houston.

CEFT strongly influenced the teaching of Czech in Texas high schools, colleges, and universities during the 1950s, 1960s, and early 1970s. Scholarships were awarded to students of the language, and several of these students went on to obtain advanced degrees in Slavic languages, while others accepted civilian or military linguistic positions with the United States government. Dr. Skrivanek himself built up the Czech program at Texas A&M University, and the development of the Czech language program stimulated the growth of a Russian language program there as well.

At Texas A&M, Dr. Skrivanek developed a textbook and audio-tape program entitled *Conversational Czech*, which was adopted by language programs in other institutions. He also assisted J. L. Chervenka, Sr. in establishing a Czech language program at Rogers High School, at that time the only program of its kind in the United States. As the number of Czech programs in Texas educational institutions increased, Dr. Skrivanek led the instructors in affiliating with the Houston Area Teachers of Foreign Languages, which organized a Slavic Languages Section.

Dr. Skrivanek also helped to establish cultural ties between the Czechs in Texas and Czechoslovak institutions which survive to the present day. After spending a year's leave at Charles University in Prague, Czechoslovakia, Dr. Skrivanek was instrumental in arranging a year-long visit to Texas by the Czech scholar Václav Hunáček of Charles University as a guest of the Texas Educational Agency. He also laid the groundwork for a summer study program designed for Czech instructors and other interested parties from the state of Texas at Charles University in Prague. Although Dr. Skrivanek died before his plans could be realized, his brother Joseph J. Skrivanek later served as the first director of such a program, in cooperation with the Czechoslovak Institute of Foreign Affairs, and this program, in a reorganized form, is still in existence.

Like other ethnic groups in Texas and across the nation, the Texas Czechs began to increase their activities in the late 1960s, and a general growth in ethnic awareness continued into the 1970s. Czech-American celebrations such as Westfest and the Ennis Polka Festival became ever more popular, and new events were added in communities across the state, as fraternal organizations became more active in promoting Czech language and culture in state schools. Other support groups, such as CESAT, were revived. However, CEFT itself entered into a stage of relative inactivity after the death, on December 27, 1972, of Dr. Skrivanek, its guiding light. Co-founder Henry R. Maresh had died in 1957, and August Kacir died in 1973.

In the mid-1980s, however, CEFT emerged as a re-energized organization that was to successfully complete one of the most important projects in the history of the Czech community in Texas. At this time, the organization was led by President Joseph J. Skrivanek, the brother of John M. Skrivanek, and Vice-President Cyril (Sid) Pokladnik, another long-time member of the organization, along with Tim Kostom, R. J. (Rudy) Sefcik, Mrs. John M. (Lil) Skrivanek, and Mrs. Benita Pavlu. Among the newly elected directors were Louis Hanus, Marvin J. Marek, Albert J. Blaha, Calvin C. Chervenka, Victor A. Peter, Jan Vaculik, Bishop John Morkovsky, Rev. Henry A. Beseda, Sidney Kacir, Steve Shiller,

Amos Pavlik, and Jerry D. Odstrcil. Marvin J. Marek served as the new secretary, Sidney Kacir as legal advisor, Rudy Sefcik as English-language publicity director, and Jan Vaculik as Czech-language publicity director.

Meeting in early 1985, the CEFT officers and directors decided to organize a drive to establish a Czech Chair at either the University of Texas at Austin or Texas A&M University. An endowed chair of Czech Language and Literature, or of Czech Studies, had long been a dream among Texas-Czech leaders. Although the Czech language had been taught at the University of Texas at Austin continuously since 1926, even that program seemed to have an uncertain future in the eighties, and Czech programs at other universities—like that at Texas A&M—had been discontinued. The goal of CEFT was to establish a strong institutional base with independent funding to insure that basic Czech language courses would be offered from semester to semester on a regular basis. CEFT would then ensure that resources would be available to build a total academic program—both on the undergraduate and the graduate levels—that would be competitive with major Slavic language programs throughout the United States. Initial contacts with officials from the University of Texas and Texas A&M University led to expressions of interest from both institutions.

President Skrivanek called for a major organizational meeting at the Supreme lodge of the SPJST in Temple, Texas, on March 1, 1986. Not only CEFT representatives, but delegates from all organizations associated in any way with Texas Czechs, and any other interested individuals, were invited to attend, along with deans and other representatives from both the University of Texas and Texas A&M. The general enthusiasm expressed for a fund raising project at this meeting encouraged the CEFT officers and directors to continue their efforts. It became apparent that Texas Czechs from a broad spectrum of fraternal and religious groups were willing to cooperate in the project.

CEFT, once again an active organization, began to hold frequent meetings, and the drive to fund the Czech Chair was publicized throughout the state. Many of the largest donations in 1986 were made by the CEFT officers themselves, and fraternal and other organizations began to pledge large sums as well. The goal was to collect $500,000, with the expectation that the University receiving the endowment would match this figure, for a total endowment of one million dollars. As early as January 1985, a few individuals had already begun to make pledges toward a possible endowment. At a CEFT meeting in Ennis on May 3, 1986, it was reported that about $102,000 had been raised in pledges and actual donations. Later that year, on November 16, a meeting was held in conjunction with the Sesquicentennial Celebration entitled "Czech Music in Texas" in Bryan, Texas, an event which itself functioned as a CEFT fund-raiser. By this time, over $125,000 was committed to the endowment, and Ben Trcalek of Caldwell was appointed treasurer of the organization, assuming the financial duties that had been carried out until then by President Skrivanek. (After Mr. Trcalek's death, the position of treasurer was taken over by Mr. Trcalek's son Ben, Jr.) At a meeting on January 31, 1987, it was reported that nearly $175,000 in cash and pledges had been raised. During 1987 Glen Hutka and Laddie A. Matula, Sr. joined the board of directors.

Although the rate of donations and pledges declined during 1987, by January 1988 the total was over $200,000. In 1988 Roger Kolar and I joined the board of directors. CEFT intensified its publicity efforts with press releases and a brochure designed for mass distribution.

By the end of 1988, only about half of the goal of $500,000 had been met, but a major breakthrough in the fund-raising campaign came in early 1989. At a meeting on March 4, at RVOS headquarters in Temple, Mr. Skrivanek announced that—after preliminary contacts made by Sid Pokladnik and Calvin Chervenka with Al Kercho of Fort Worth—Patrick Patek, president of the Stephen and Mary Birch Foundation of Wilmington, Delaware, had indicated that a substantial contribution to the endowment fund was imminent. The Birch Foundation had tentatively agreed to pledge approximately $200,000, assuring that the goal for the endowment could be met in the near future. Negotiations concerning matching funds and other issues were reopened with both target universities. Discussions with the Birch Foundation continued, with Sidney Kacir taking an active part. At the same time CEFT adopted a new set of by-laws which refined and clarified the form and functions of the organization and which made it more efficient in administering the endowment. The process of organizing a master list of donors to CEFT was begun, and Howard Leshikar, president of the fraternal organization SPJST, was elected to serve as a new director at a May 1989 meeting.

By March of 1990, a final agreement had been reached with the Birch Foundation, and negotiations with the two universities were intensified. Under the provisions of the new by-laws, Roger Kolar was elected chairman of the board, and Calvin Chervenka, vice-chairman. On May 1, 1990, Chairman Kolar and President Skrivanek signed a letter of agreement with William H. Cunningham, president of the University of Texas at Austin, outlining the provisions for an endowed chair to be named the "Texas Chair in Czech Studies," and which would represent a commitment to Czech language, literature, and culture, in perpetuity. With matching funds from UT, this Chair, the only one of its kind in the United States, was eventually funded for one million dollars. The agreement was ratified by the CEFT directors at a meeting in La Grange, on May 19, 1990. The University Board of Regents ratified the agreement at its meeting of June 14, 1990.

President Skrivanek, who had lived to see the realization of the project to which he had dedicated himself for so many years, died on February 1, 1991. CEFT lives on, and our current project of establishing the CEFT Czech Fellowship at Texas A&M University is in the spirit of our founders. This program will: 1) bring advanced graduate students from two Moravian universities to Texas A&M; 2) establish Czech language classes at Texas A&M for students and members of the general public; 3) provide Czech-to-English translation services for the Texas Czech community; 4) provide assistance to Czech-American historical and cultural groups in Texas; and 5) encourage ties between the State of Texas and the Czech Republic. Our goal is within reach: over $150,000 of the $250,000 required to establish the CEFT Czech Fellowship at Texas A&M has already been raised. With the continued generosity of donors who share our goals of strengthening the study of Czech language and culture in Texas institutions of higher learning, the CEFT Czech Fellowship at Texas A&M can be in place by the Fall semester of 1999.

Subject: Conversation with Czechoslovak President

(Reports on T. G. Masaryk in the American Diplomatic Correspondence in Prague)

Milada Polišenská

President T. G. Masaryk: it is easy to call to mind the well-known picture of this charismatic, broadly respected and, by many, beloved man. Many of those who have met him or worked with him have shared their fascination by publishing their experience. Of course, the task of the diplomat is to be an analytical, critical, and objective observer and informer. Diplomatic reports are not about friendships with interesting personalities. But they are meant to help their governments in foreign policy decisions. The diplomatic reports later became diplomatic records, and as such, help researchers in their search for deeper insight and broader perspective. Therefore, I have been interested in how President Masaryk was viewed from the American diplomatic perspective, and am very happy to have the opportunity to share with you my results. This paper is a part of my larger research project on Czechoslovak-U.S. diplomatic relations from 1918. It is based on the reports of the U.S. Legation in Prague to the Department of State, which are deposited in the National Archives in Washington, D.C., and, for context, also on the Crane Papers, deposited in the Special Collections of Georgetown University.

During Masaryk's Presidency (1918-35), five successive American ministers led the American Legation in Prague. The

first U.S. minister was Richard Crane, serving at this post from
1919 to 1921. In July 1919 he summarized the results he had
achieved, and described the problems he had had to face during
his first two months of work in Prague:

> Of course, as is natural in a new republic, things are very much
> disorganized. The new government is exceedingly weak in mat-
> ters of administration. In fact, the President told me that this
> would be a very difficult matter to overcome, as, previous to the
> revolution, it had been the aim of the Czechs to disorganize the
> government services in order to break down the Austro-
> Hungarian regime, and now it is necessary to re-educate these
> people to work along constructive lines.

Crane also reports that "[Masaryk] made a very significant address on the Fourth of July, in which he referred to his admiration
for America and his attempt to use American principles of democracy as far as possible for his work here." In the context of a
difficult domestic political situation and Masaryk's prestige and
authority, according to Crane, the president could have even
assumed dictatorial powers: "President Masaryk is above party,
and as proof of this, the Socialists accuse him of being a bourgeois, and the bourgeois accuse him of being a radical. There
seems to be a disposition on the part of everyone to grant him as
much power as possible." [13]
    On August 14, 1919, Crane reported about the arrival of
Herbert Hoover, the future U.S. president, who worked for the
American Relief Administration. On this occasion, relations
between Czechoslovakia and Hungary were discussed: "The conference with President Masaryk on Sunday was more illuminating,
and though the President was reserved at first, he finally came out
with his real opinion, i.e., that if the Hapsburgs should go on the
throne in Hungary it meant a move in that direction in Vienna and
this would spread to Germany and surround Czechoslovakia with
a network of monarchist intrigues." [14] Crane reported, in this context, that T. G. Masaryk discussed an economic rapprochement
between the Danubian states, and received Mihaly Karolyi and the
Hungarian Social Democrat Diner-Denes several times, "but there
is a good deal of speculation about the real object of their pro-
tracted stay here. One of them is that Tusar has sold out, and is

making arrangements with the Magyars, contrary to the wishes of Masaryk, who uses the Danubian confederation discussions as a mask and does not want to break openly with his Premier".[15]

T. G. Masaryk always paid deep attention to Russia, and his prestige as the best specialist available in Slavic and particularly Russian questions opened the door of the White House for him in 1918. According to Crane, "Masaryk feels that the Bolsheviks are likely to remain in power for some time principally because opponents cannot unite on a policy. Masaryk consistently maintains that the Social Revolutionist Party, because of its hold on the Russian peasant, is the most likely to succeed the Bolshevists. It is logical, therefore, that this party should make Prague its headquarters, which I am reliably informed it has done."[16] Crane reported in this context the repeated visits of Kerensky in Prague and about the activities of the organization Volya Rossii. Crane also reported in detail on Masaryk's public speeches and interviews on topics such as bolshevism, or the critical situation within the Social Democratic Party.[17]

In 1921 President Masaryk was seriously ill. Crane's reports evidenced how much the illness of the President influenced the domestic political situation. In particular, Crane was critical of the fact that no measures to appoint a vice-president were being taken at that time. The first considerations about what would happen in case of Masaryk's resignation or death appeared not only in the diplomatic correspondence, but also in the mass media. The *New York Times* reported Masaryk's resignation on April 22, 1921, and had to withdraw the report on the next day. T. G. Masaryk overcame this critical period. However, the condition of his health would be an important topic in diplomatic correspondence for almost fifteen years.

The personal bonds between the two generations of Cranes and two generations of Masaryks resulted in a certain level of informal contacts and communication.[18] Moreover, Richard Crane's reports were to be received by men who had known T. G. Masaryk just a few years before, in 1918, when recognition of an independent Czechoslovakia was discussed, by Secretary of State Robert Lansing in particular. Lansing, but also American President Woodrow Wilson, had in their hands the best references and recommendations on T. G. Masaryk. Therefore it is not too surprising that Crane, in his correspondence, did not consider it necessary to report on T. G. Masaryk as a person, and the Department of State did not instruct him to do so.

Lewis Einstein, the next American minister in Prague after Crane, submitted his credentials in 1921. With his nine years of service in Prague up to 1930, he was the longest-serving U.S. head of the diplomatic mission in Czechoslovakia. Prague was the last diplomatic post in Einstein's long career, which had started in the very beginning of the twentieth century and included U.S. legations in Constantinople, Peking, and Sophia. Lewis Einstein was the author of a number of studies and books, including his memoirs, *A Diplomat Looks Back*.[19] The only available American diplomatic memoirs from Prague are Einstein's chapter, along with the well-known *Memoirs* and *From Prague after Munich* by George F. Kennan.[20] Lewis Einstein's portait of Masaryk is one of the most detailed and complex ever published. I believe it should be included in my presentation, even though it was not written on the official legation stationery. How did Lewis Einstein look back at T. G. Masaryk? He appreciated very much the moral qualities of the Czechoslovak President. He was, however, in some respects not only critical, but even a little ironical, though this did not diminish his high opinion of Masaryk's personality and ideas.

> Masaryk himself preferred an American standard of simplicity, he not infrequently would walk to the Legation to have a quiet chat with me. He detested every kind of pomp and his personal character was not affected by his sudden elevation to the highest dignity.
>
> The positiveness of the opinions he expressed seemed to me to come more from his training as an educator than from his position as Chief of State. So far as I could judge, his literary style was steeped with the jargon of the German university. Earlier writings, like his book on Russia, which he gave me, are full of those long and ugly half-philosophical, half-mystical words which learned Germans delight to parade and the ponderous vagueness of which contributes so often to their reputation for depth.
>
> As President Masaryk gained in political wisdom he gradually discarded much of this Teutonic vocabulary and shook off some of his earlier academic inheritance. His attitude also

became more tolerant toward everyone except perhaps university professors.

I believe that his greatest merit was to preserve the liberal spirit undimmed and stamp this on the new state during the black reaction which left democracy tottering in central Europe. When I sat down to chat with the President in his study at Lány, it was hard to imagine the wild adventures which this kind-looking, quiet old man had gone through in creating the new state. The principal impression he made on me was one of natural dignity. He seemed to have none of that compelling force which made anyone who fell under the spell of Theodore Roosevelt ready to follow him as a leader, right or wrong. The principal impression he made on me was one of natural dignity.

Masaryk's strength seemed to me to lie rather in a quiet reserve of moral force, a shyness with authority, and an inherent goodness which was simple without being gullible. His verbal expression was even a little elementary. He repeated truisms, and his outlook seemed to men neither original nor striking, although occasionally his insight cut deep below the surface. He neither strove for effect nor did he seem to care if he created any impression on his listener. He was more human and less of a superman th   I had anticipated. There was no trace of affectation or vanity in his speech. Underneath this homely benevolence ran a strain of what for want of a better name can be called idealistic opportunism. I suspect that his most important decisions were taken in the silence of his thought by moral instinct more than by reason. To me he observed that there was something in the Czech character which courts martyrdom, and in saying this he may have had himself in mind, for there was a touch of John Huss in his soul.

There was nothing histrionic about Masaryk, not even glibness, nor any trace of the politician's tricks. His handshake was not hearty, and it was impossible to imagine him striving for popularity by any cheap devices. But his outspokenness was engaging, and I admired the profound sincerity of a man who had enough of moral courage to refuse to flatter the natural pride of his people and appeared far more inclined to criticize than to praise them. This was nothing new, for on two occasions before the war he had made himself the most hated man in Bohemia.[21]

President Masaryk's name is invariably associated with that of Dr. Beneš. At the beginning of his administration, when the President fell gravely ill and believed he would die, he called the political leaders to his bedside and asked them to give their solemn pledge to elect Beneš as his successor. His opinion never changed in this respect. Yet intellectually the two men were very different, and temperamentally I suspect Masaryk to have been the younger, for under his calm appearance lay hidden a still youthful fire.[22]

Eduard Beneš was connected with T. G. Masaryk in many ways, including attempts on his life. As Einstein confidentially reported to the Department of State, Beneš had told him, that on four different occasions the organization "Awakening Hungarians" had sent assassins to kill T. G. Masaryk and Beneš himself. The affair was not given any publicity since Beneš and Masaryk wanted Czechoslovakia to avoid being connected with any political criminality.[23]

Lewis Einstein reported regularly on Masaryk's press interviews and speeches such as those against fascism and analyzed Masaryk's activities related to the presidential elections in 1926 — unfortunately, my limited time does not allow me to pay more attention to them.

Einstein's successor at the ministerial post in Prague was Abraham Ratshesky, a businessman and philanthropist from Boston. He served in Prague for three years, from 1930 to 1933. After his resignation, Francis White was appointed in Prague, but he spent just one year at this post and was replaced in 1934 by J. Butler Wright. Among the files of diplomatic correspondence sent from Prague under Ratshesky and White, I did not find any reports or dispatches with a more specific focus on T. G. Masaryk.

The steady flow of reports on the Czechoslovak president started again under J. Butler Wright. The content of those reports changed drastically. Now, in the middle of the 1930s, the American minister had only to report on the seriously ill health of the eighty-five-year-old President, his declining vitality, his resignation which appeared to be inevitable, and the crucial question: who would be going "in the Castle," and who would replace Beneš "in Černín," if Masaryk's wish to be succeeded by Beneš would be fulfilled? The reports of the American diplomat show the respect and compassion for T. G. Masaryk and his family, but document also how Wright noticed the negative aspects of the prolongation of the decision, the uncertain future of Czechoslovakia, the grow-ing political maneuvering, and the lack of information, but in par-ticular the semi-paralysis of many governmental activities requir-ing the participation and signature of the Chief Executive.

> The prolonged anxiety is evident from the fact that his son, Mr. John Masaryk, Minister at London, is in this country more fre-quently and for longer periods than formerly; that he or his sis-ter Alice are never absent from Lány at the same time; that the presentation of the new Spanish Minister was deferred for some weeks, notwithstanding official assurances that the President's health continued [to be] satisfactory. From John Masaryk comes a slightly more frank admission that those nearest to him are prepared for "anything at anytime." From the Editor-in-Chief of the *Prager Presse* I gain the information that the situa-tion is disturbing and far from satisfactory. And from John O. Crane I learn confidentially that the President is now able to read but little and therefore depends largely upon those who read aloud to him, and while able to conduct the final revision of the last volume of his memoirs, his condition is certainly not such as properly befits the Chief of State of a nation like Czechoslovakia at the present time.

This is the summary of information by Minister Wright from July 25, 1935.[24] In September of 1935, Wright reported,[25] that "the domestical situation of Czechoslovakia clearly crystallizes into two parts: first the health of the President and the selection of his successor, second is the increasing potency of the German-speak-ing element." On October 31, 1935,[26] "nothing has as yet been def-initely decided concerning the possible withdrawal of President Masaryk of his office." This difficult situation was certainly not caused by the president, but by the long and unproductive negotia-tions within the governmental coalition about the expected vacan-cies, including the post of prime minister and minister of foreign affairs.

One of the first reports Wright sent into the Department of State in the beginning of 1936 confirms that the new Czechoslo-vak President Edvard Beneš had begun his duties. After consider-ing who would be the next Czechoslovak foreign minister, the diplomat wrote without concealing his pleasure:

The health of ex-President Masaryk has undergone a marked improvement. His mind is as active as ever, his hours of work in his private library have apparently increased and he passes more time out of doors, thus fulfilling the prediction of his physician who told me personally that he confidently expected this improvement in the President's condition as soon as he was relieved from the annoyances of decisions in party politics which have in recent months exerted a particularly irritating influence upon him.[27]

It is very nice, indeed, that the last diplomatic report about T. G. Masaryk I have studied in the National Archives in Washington, D.C. describes him the way I have quoted. During those days when the Governmental coalition negotiated on his resignation and the changes in the Government positions, and when the health of the president was the topic number one, when the anxiety and pressure influenced Masaryk's environment and was certainly not beneficial to him, nobody expected such a recovery. His physical and mental strength, however, were exceptional. T. G. Masaryk had almost two more years of life ahead of him, but he disappeared from the pages of diplomatic reports, since the attention of diplomats turned toward the growing political tensions.

Minister Wright served in Prague up to 1937. His successor at the U.S. Legation in Prague was Wilbur Carr, the last American minister in Prague before the Munich Dictate.[28] Wilbur Carr was called "the Architect of American Foreign Service." Prague was his very first, and at the same time, his last diplomatic post abroad. Carr reached Prague on September 7, 1937, just a few days before Masaryk's death. One of his first duties was to attend the funeral services of the late ex-president. For Carr his Prague appointment meant the conclusion of his professional career. It was also the conclusion of one specific chapter of Czechoslovak history: Masarykian Czechoslovakia.

Texas Czech:
An Ethnolinguistic Study*

Ludmila Dutková

Summary. Guided by my main inquiry into the role that an obsolescing language remains to play in the immigrant community and in the shifting definitions of its members' ethnic identity, my ethnolinguistic fieldwork in rural Czech communities located in the Dallas-Houston-Corpus Christi triangle of Texas, mainly in Granger (Williamson Co.), and West (McLennan Co.), explored what it means to be a Texas Czech (*TxCz*) and the role of language use in this identity. Community members' perception of Czechness in self and others motivates forms of intergenerational transmission of Czech and shifting definitions of a Czech "speak-

---

*This essay describes research toward a doctoral dissertation at the University of Arizona, Tucson. My project has been funded by the National Science Foundation (Gr. No. SBR-9709262), the Wenner-Gren Foundation for Anthropological Research (Gr. No. 6213), the Czech Ex-Students Association of Texas (CESAT), Texans of Czech Ancestry (TOCA), and by individual contributions received from Texas Czechs and other interested Texans. I wish to extend my sincere thanks to them as well as to others who have provided me with accommodation, or have helped me out in other ways, mainly with transportation and further contacts. Their hospitality, generosity, and interest have meant a lot for the success of my field work. Last but not least, I want to thank all my informants for their invaluable input, and to everybody who has taken the time to fill out my lengthy questionnaire.

er." My Texas informants grew up in the 1930s, the "golden years" of American Czech (*AmCz*) (Kučera 1989), and experienced the language revival efforts in the early 1980s (Machann & Mendl 1983). A survey of community views on such efforts allows an opportunity to examine their impact on the community members' self- and other-perceived identity, as well as their language skills and attitudes. My goal is to assess the current state of *TxCz* in relationship to the self-defined identities of its speakers, and formulate an informed hypothesis about its future.

My six-month fieldwork (May–December 1997) in Texas-Czech communities followed the research design proposed in this paper.

I. Theoretical Orientation and Background

I. A. Language Death as a Field of Study. It is a fact that languages are dying. "In the last five hundred years about half the known languages of the world have disappeared" (Sasse 1992a). Krauss (1992) estimates that intergenerational transmission has been discontinued in 149 out of 187 languages of the United States and Canada. Yet the history of language death as a recognized field of study is relatively short, dating back to the 1970s. While a theory on language death is yet to be formulated (Sasse 1992a), the pioneering research and theoretical work of the 1970s and the early 1980s on languages in contact, intergenerational language shift, and community language death (e.g., Dorian 1981; Gal 1979; Haugen 1969; Hill 1973, 1977, 1978, 1983; Hill & Hill 1978, 1986; Schmidt 1985; Weinreich 1968) has since grown into a solid body of work on structural changes in dying languages in the U.S. (e.g., Campbell & Muntzel 1989; Sasse 1992b; Silva-Corvalan 1994). Polinsky (1995), for example, noting significant amounts of uniformity in structural attrition across several immigrant languages, distinguishes between dying languages and *reduced* language varieties in immigrant communities. This distinction is instrumental to this project, which defines *TxCz* as a reduced immigrant variety of Moravian Czech.

I. B. Theoretical Framework of the Project. Just as important as the structural work however, and not enough emphasized, has been work on sociocultural factors leading to language death, with few studies answering Gal's (1979) call for what Woolard (1989) succinctly defines as making "the speaker central to our thinking" (Dorian 1981; Gal 1979, 1989; Haugen 1989; Hill & Hill 1986; Hill 1985, 1989; Kulick 1992). Yet we need to be concerned with the speakers' social identities inside and outside their community, and with "why and how . . . people come to interpret their lives in such a way that they abandon one of their languages" (Kulick 1992). Therefore, the theoretical framework for my project emphasizes such (*1*) *speaker-centered* studies on language death, and it integrates research (*2*) on the *semi-speaker* phenomenon (Dorian 1977; Schmidt 1985; Smith 1992ms), (*3*) on the forms of *discontinued language transmission* (Fishman 1991a; Kulick 1992); and (*4*) on *language and ethnicity* (e.g., Fishman 1985, 1989; Gudykunst ed. 1988; Haarmann 1986; Hannan, 1996a, 1996b; Papademetre 1994).

(1-2) Centering on speakers means viewing "human actors rather than personified languages" as "the active agents" (Woolard 1989) in the processes of language shift and loss. Gal's (1979) ethnographic microstudy of the social circumstances of language shift in the Austrian village of Oberwart and Dorian's (1981) monograph on language death among East Sutherland Gaelic speakers were the first to rely heavily on participant observation, the approach central to this project. By entering local social networks, Gal (1979) was able to identify the "impression management" linking the speaker's patterns of language choice with their interlocutor's identity and status. With the redistribution of functions between the dying Hungarian and thriving German, Hungarian, associated with peasant status, attained the symbolic value of a "solidarity code," while German, the language of education and social mobility, became valued as a "power code." Further, participant observation led Dorian (1981) to discover the semi-speaker phenomenon and the power of receptive competence, allowing semi-speakers with low productive competence to effectively interact with fluent Gaelic speakers and be perceived as equally capable interlocutors. By "making the speaker central to our thinking," Dorian showed the role of stigmatized ethnic identity in the language shift, identified the solidarity function of

Gaelic, assessed the role of language attitudes and loyalty, and suggested age grouping rather than commonly acknowledged social stratification as affecting language choice. Her critical evaluation of the data obtained from self-reports elicited in the form of a questionnaire is methodologically valuable to this project.

Among other research which has focused on individual speakers, Hill's (e.g., 1985, 1989) and Hill & Hill's (e.g., 1986) research on Nahuatl (Mexicano), a Uto-Aztecan language spoken in Malinche Volcano regional towns of central Mexico, discovered a functional split in "narrow honorific speakers" (NHSs) as opposed to "broad honorific speakers," in the use of Mexicano inside and outside the community, as revealing of the more or less advanced stage of language shift in these individual speakers, and identified the conflict caused by puristic attitudes of NHSs. Also Schmidt's (1985) monograph on reduced Dyirbal of young speakers (YD) in the Jambun community at Murray Upper in the Australian Queensland, demonstrates how the older speakers' evaluations of YD as "imperfect" (i.e., by insiders) reinforce stigmatization of Dyirbal by whites (i.e., outsiders), and how their puristic "corrective mechanism" only speeds up the replacement of Dyirbal by English. These studies show that what is accepted as a language, and who is accepted as its speakers, is negotiated within the shifting community itself, and that speakers' attempts to create and maintain certain identity are undermined by the dominant society which perceives them as "pathological" (Hill 1993). Finally, Kulick (1992), through his participant observation in the Papua New Guinean village of Gapun, observed that it was not the concept of stigmatized ethnic identity (as in Dorian), but the difference between "backward" villagers (speaking only Taiap, the local vernacular) and "civilized" villagers (speaking both Taiap and Tok Pisin of whites), that played a crucial role in the language shift. This brief review supports my belief that a full interpretation of linguistic data is possible only if they are viewed in both the light of the complexities of speakers' real lives and the shifts "in personal and group values and goals" (Kulick 1992).

(3) The study of child language socialization has often neglected social motivation for discontinued language transmission beyond the decisions parents make for their children, and the influence of caretakers and siblings. For example, Dopke (1986) and

Fantini (1985) suggest that the kinds of input and reactions in languages that children receive from their bilingual parents decide which language is acquired. More recent studies have emphasized that children are socialized through interaction (Ochs 1988; Schieffelin and Ochs 1986; Schieffelin 1990). One important point beyond these findings comes from Kulick's (1992: 24) observations of interaction among Gapun villagers, and between focal children and their parents: rather than a conscious decision by adults to stop transmitting Taiap to their children, their "thoughts on language, children, and self all work to systematically bias their language practices in favor of Tok Pisin." Inspired by his work, my project considers the ideological bases of intergenerational language transmission.

(4) Finally, despite the interest in the study of ethnic identity in contemporary anthropology and the scholarship of social science (e.g., Banks & Gay 1978; Bank 1996; Barkan 1995), a relatively small body of research has explored language and ethnicity among speakers of dying languages in the U.S. immigrant communities (e.g., Fishman 1985, 1989, 1991a, 1991b; Haugen 1969). Although we know that language is an essential part of speakers' identities (Brenzinger & Dimmendaal 1992), we have not come to fully understand how people think of themselves "in relation to one another and to their changing social world," and how what they think is "encoded and mediated through language" (Kulick 1992: 9). The present study should contribute to our understanding of this issue from the perspective of language change, its roots, and consequences.

I. C. Research on American Czech and Texas Czech. The study of linguistic and social factors in *AmCz* (Eckert 1987, 1988, 1990; Henzl 1975ms, 1981; Kochis 1980; Kučera 1989), has emphasized "attrition of form" rather than "functional attrition" (Hill 1993). Likewise, the research on *TxCz*, has mainly focused on its historical Moravian dialectical features (Hannan 1992; Mendl 1976ms; Perkowski 1976) and linguistic description (Eckert 1993, 1997; Kutac 1967ms; Kučera 1989; Smith 1992ms). For example, Henzl (1975ms) explored the effect of active cultivation of literary Czech by its immigrant speakers and their maintenance of this "specific dialectal variety of the Czech language." Based on the analysis of speech (spontaneous and elicited) and questionnaire data from eighty-four informants living in California, Illinois, and New York, Henzl concluded that the amount of formal education in Czech, ties with the original country, and language attitudes were crucial to the maintenance of literary Czech by *AmCz* speakers. Valuable to my project, Henzl's work attempted to establish the causative link between *social* conditions and language change in *AmCz* communities. In another study, Mendl (1976ms) analyzed the speech of four *TxCz* speakers, using the patterns of historical phonological development of the Czech vowel system as a criterion to determine their dialects as Czech or Moravian. He defines *TxCz* as a "mixture of different dialects" in one speaker's idiolect, resulting from their active participation in Czech social, religious, and fraternal life throughout Texas. Mendl's method of searching for dialectal distinctions has been helpful to the structural portion of my data analysis. Further, Kučera (1989), using oral and written data from more than 200 Czech-Americans, distinguishes between changes in language features as a result of relaxation in language norm, *atrophy*, and the process of *Americanization* via replacement or enrichment of the reduced language. If Henzl's (1975ms) project is according to her "the first systematic analysis" of *AmCz*, Kučera's study appears to be the most complete survey of current features of *AmCz* today. Also his work aids my structural analysis of data. Finally, Smith's (1992ms) descriptive analysis of linguistic variation of *TxCz* among three age groups in two *TxCz* communities showed that informants in their fifties retained lexical and morphological patterns far better than the lower age groups. His *TxCz* semi-speaker continuum, and Eckert's (1993) identification of features for each stage of gradual loss of Czech, based on her analysis of the tombstone inscriptions at the graveyard in Praha, Texas, provide additional tools for the section of my data analysis aimed to assess the current state of *TxCz*. These studies are usually prefaced by a historical background for the Czech immigration as it relates to the development of *AmCz*. However, there is no study of either American or Texan Czechs that would provide insights into the community members' own perceptions of what it means to be an American or Texan Czech. Therefore, a different, ethnolinguistic and speaker-centered perspective of my project usefully intersects with these descriptive studies, with the potential to capture yet more fully the Czech language experience in the U.S.

I. D. Czech Immigration to the U.S. and the Decline of Czech. Both religious and economic factors, the latter particularly between 1848 and World War I, impelled the migration of Czechs and Moravians to America (Henzl 1981; Machann & Mendl 1983). Most of Czech immigration came to Texas from the former territory of the Austro-Hungarian Empire. The history and politics of Moravian separatism in their homeland (Hannan, 1996a), and the fact that nearly 80% of the Czech immigrants to Texas came from the Lachian and Wallachian regions of Moravia (Janak 1985, 1991), partly explain the complexity of the Czech ethnic identity in Texas, and distinguish this from other *AmCz* communities. From the 1850s till World War II, the district chain migration (Robek 1979) continued to thrive with new waves of immigration (6,000 immigrants a year in 1920-1940), which dropped to 6,023 immigrants total in 1981-1990, and a mere 1,000 in 1993 (U.S. Census). In 1990, Czechs comprised only 0.5% of the immigrant population in the U.S. (with 191,754 Texans of Czech ancestry), 24.8% less than in 1980.

The migration pattern is reflected in the life cycle of *AmCz*, with its "golden years" in 1890s-1930s, and a gradual decline since the 1940s (Kučera 1989). Incomplete acquisition of Czech and highly variable proficiency among *TxCz* speakers began in the second generation. Since the 1940s, *TxCz*, merely the "kitchen language" for its speakers (Hannan 1996a), has undergone a *gradual* death (Campbell & Muntzel 1989). The "ethnic enclosure" (Hewitt 1979) of early rural communities has gradually dissolved, and over the years, both decreased immigration from, and weakened ties with, Czechoslovakia (now the Czech Republic), then a part of the Eastern Bloc (1950s-1980s), have diminished chances for language reinforcement. For example, in Ellis County in the 1970s, Czech was spoken by the first-generation Czechs, and only rarely used by the second-generation Czechs (Splawn 1972ms). Yet, that even second-generation Czechs in Fayette, Austin, and Washington counties were often fluent in Czech, English, and due to the coexistence with Texan-German ethnic communities, in

German (Machann & Mendl 1983), shows that we need to aim at identifying locally specific factors which are the roots of variable maintenance of Czech across *TxCz* communities.

The relationship between ethnicity and religion is relevant to understanding of the assimilation process of Czechs in Texas. "Ethnoreligion," essential to self-identity of the first generation, became ambivalent for the second generation, as the "swect mother tongue" of Sunday schools till the mid 1920s, changed into a "stumbling block" with the rise of assimilationism in the 1940s, and then revived in the third, well-secured generation of American Czechs (Machalek 1979).

The history of the *TxCz* immigration and community has been well documented (Hewitt 1978ms; Machann 1976; Machann ed. 1979; Machann & Mendl 1983; Maresh & Hudson 1934; Maresh 1946; Stasney 1938ms). Taking a sociological perspective, Polasek (1979) renders early life in Moravia, and Skrabanek (1979, 1988) portrays social life in his hometown of Snook, Texas, remembering "Tex-Czech," the language of his childhood, and importantly, the sharp "we vs. others" distinction pervasive in the 1930s.

The emergence of "new ethnicity" and ethnolinguistic revival movement in the early 1970s (Banks & Gay 1978; Fishman 1991a) gained urgency for *TxCz* in the early 1980s (Machann 1976), with nostalgia growing among the old generations (*Věstník* Jan. 2, 1972). Among Texas scholars, Machann (1976) describes the bleak prospects of *TxCz*, calling for a "Czech renaissance," and research "dealing with attitudes [to] language acquisition and retention," while Mendl (1976ms) observes "a revival in the interest of Czech" at that time. Two decades later, Hannan (1992) seconds Machann's call for research on *TxCz* while the language is still alive.

II. Specific Objectives

I adopt Gal's (1979) view of speech as a social activity, exploring the relationship between the culture of language and its form. To show how shifting of speakers' attitudes relates to shifting in their language use patterns, I approach language shift as a socially motivated change (Ibid.), and as cultural reproduction (Kulick 1992). The research question central to my inquiry is, *What role does an obsolescent language continue to play in the immigrant community and in the shifting definitions of its members' ethnic identity?* Specifically, (1) How is the *TxCz* speech community defined? (2) What does it mean to be a speaker of a language, i.e., a speaker of Texas Czech / Moravian? (3) What motivates the discontinued intergenerational transmission of Czech? (4) What are the contexts of use of *TxCz*, and the role of language use in the speaker's identity? (5) If heightened consciousness of having Moravian ancestry has persisted, is the speakers' identity still manifested by Moravian dialectical features in their idiolects? And, (6) what are the attitudes toward the revival of Czech among *TxCz* speakers and English monolinguals of Czech descent?

Speech communities (e.g., Dorian 1982; Gumperz 1986; Labov 1972; Schmidt 1985) are locally constructed, just as the concept of a language speaker is "constructed in the speech community through ongoing negotiations among its members" (Hill & Hill 1986). When languages are dying, it may become increasingly difficult to determine who is a speaker of the language — not only for outsiders, but also for the community members themselves (Romaine 1989). How to adequately describe a community of *TxCz* speakers who display different levels of productive and receptive competence in Czech? Similar to Dorian (1982), my working definition of *TxCz* community draws on Hymes' (1974: 47) proposal to consider a social group with "the entire organization of linguistic means within it," and Corder's (1973: 53; italics in the original) view that "a speech community is made up of people who *regard themselves* as speaking the same language" with no "other defining attributes." My concern is to understand how the nature of speech community might be contested and problematized by its members. Questions one to three address this and other issues, such as self-perceived and "other-perceived" language proficiency, i.e. the *TxCz* speaker as a community-defined concept; categories of "speakers"; and discontinued language transmission. In the process of shift, language functions become redistributed and those of the dying language, reduced (for *AmCz*, Kučera, 1989).

Question four targets the functional contexts that help untangle the multiple composition of a speaker's identity. While even the ritual function of Czech ceased with the rise of assimilationism in the 1940s, *TxCz* still serves very limited functions that must be identified, such as the marking of intimacy vs. social distance. It has been claimed that *AmCz* has lost the honorific *T/V* pronoun distinction of full Czech (Henzl 1975ms; Kučera 1989), but ways of expressing intimacy vs. distance have not been explored. Further, question five is motivated by the fact that most of the Czech immigration to Texas originated in *Lašsko* (Lachia) and *Valašsko* (Wallachia) of northeastern Moravia. Some speakers who use Moravian dialectal features even today proudly assert their Moravian identity (*"Já su Moravec"*), some speak the language but exhibit no specific Moravian ethnic consciousness, and yet others, although raised as English monolinguals, identify themselves as Moravians, Czech-Moravians, or Czechs. I explore whether these Moravian features preserve any distinctive elements of the attested historical Lachian and Wallachian dialects of Moravian Czech, as one dimension of identity. Texan bilinguals who call themselves *"Moravci"* in Czech, usually resort to the available terminology of English to define their ethnicity and language as "Czech" (Hannan 1996a). Hanak (1979) defines Texas Czechs as "Texans with difference," who have come to possess "identity with difference," as they modified, rather than altered, their self-identification. My goal is to assess applicability of these notions to Texas Czechs today.

On question six, we must remember that despite Sussex's (1982) assertion that "émigré Slavic languages have not yet reached the stage of impending language death," while Czech culture still lingers in people's everyday lives and is celebrated in traditional ethnic festivals, the studies on *TxCz* have long predicted its imminent death. Perhaps more in tune with the research findings on *AmCz* and *TxCz* is Olesch's (1970) prediction that since the number of immigrant speakers of Slavic languages had declined so dramatically until that year, the language's "extinction is almost assured." What then are the symbolic meanings of Czech for Texas Czechs today? What are the chances for language revival in Texas? Who are the community members concerned about maintaining Czech? Is more than nostalgia for the "old days" at issue? It might be possible to work toward reversing language shift (e.g., Fishman 1966, 1991a), having older speakers involved in language clubs and community-supported courses, but first we must understand the loyalty of today's *TxCz* speakers to the Czech culture *and* their heritage language—the issues I've been concerned with in this project.

Czech has an essential symbolic meaning for the grassroots community leaders and activists in *TxCz* organizations. For example, the Czech Educational Foundation of Texas (CEFT) that once succeeded in establishing the Texas Chair of Czech Studies at the University of Texas at Austin, is currently involved in fund-raising for a fellowship at Texas A&M University that would bring Moravian students to teach Czech classes and offer assistance in Czech to *TxCz* communities. The Czech Ex-Students Association (CESAT) promotes Czech studies and interest in teaching Czech in form of scholarships and petitions to local school teachers. Such activism is their way of asserting and declaring deep-rooted Czech identity (R. Kolar, C. Machann, p.c.). A search for and awareness of one's roots in the "old country" are just as important for the Czech Heritage Society of Texas (CHST). Hewitt (1978ms) defines Czech ethnicity as a synthetic product of active participation in social and religious organizations formed in the late 1880s. Even today, fraternal organizations formed in late 1880s, such as the Slavonic Benevolent Order of the State of Texas (SPJST), continue to promote Czech culture and heritage. Does the membership in Czech-related organizations make a difference in the attitudes toward the Czech language among Texan Czechs? Still contributing to language maintenance are *Našinec*, *Hospodář*, and Czech sections of *Věstník*, the only remaining Czech newspapers in Texas, although today's subscriptions to *Našinec* and *Hospodář* cannot compare to the "golden years" of *TxCz*.

III. Methods of Data Collection and Analysis

In the 1970s, the prime time of attempts to revive Czech, 94% of American Czechs lived in the communities between Dallas, Houston, and Corpus Christi (*Věstník* January 2, 1972). Two focal communities—Granger and West—were identified as

major field sites through preliminary research and already established contacts, including my summer trip to Texas. I hypothesize
that the number of speakers of Czech in a community plays a role
in the community-based definition of a *TxCz* speaker. I judge
Granger to include more speakers and West fewer; hence the importance of this comparison.

The latest study of *TxCz* communities (Smith 1992ms)
focuses on the structural language changes rather than ideological
and attitudinal questions. My method, in principle a participant
observation of family life and public occasions in both communities, aims at retrieving community members' own views. It draws
on Gal's (1979) assertion that macro-sociological processes contribute to language shift only through the speakers' (re)interpreta-
tions, reflected in their language choice, and Kulick's (1992)
emphasis on identifying the forms of language transmission, as
well as his observation of discrepancy between what speakers do
and what they *think* they do. The project combines discourse-
based, sociolinguistic, and historical methods. Specifically, it in-
volves audio-taping, ethnographic notes, library research (e.g.,
Czech archives of SPJST in Temple, Texas), and comparative
material from cataloguing Svatava Jakobson's tape collection
(1968-1985) on *TxCz*.

III. A. Discourse-based and Sociolinguistic Methods.
(1) Interviews and Naturally Occurring Conversations. I inter-
viewed both *TxCz* speakers and English monolinguals of Czech
descent in order to define community understanding of what it
means to be a Texan Czech and/or Moravian, and articulate the
community based ideological view of the significance of language
transmission. To investigate the speakers' identities and assess
their proficiency in Czech, I recorded semi-directed and naturally
occurring conversations in Czech, English, or both, among speakers themselves and between me and the speakers. I was particularly interested in their childhood memories, family histories, their
language autobiographies, recollections of the early days of the
community, school and church activities, community celebrations
and festivals, and contacts with the "old home country." I was also
concerned with their attitudes toward Czech culture, functions of

Czech, existing Czech media, and the need to retain and transmit Czech, as well as their predictions for its future.

My data analysis (in-progress) aims to further illuminate the meaning of the Texan Czech and/or Moravian identity to both community members themselves and others, and my informants' self-reflections and self-reports that bring to life their theories about how much Czech they know and how to account for the gap between their receptive and productive competence.

(2) Questionnaire on Language Use and Language Attitudes. The interviews and naturally occurring conversations helped in the revisions of my questionnaire on language use and attitudes, which I distributed to as many people in the communities as had agreed to answer it in order to obtain additional background information. Attitudinal questions in the questionnaire were complemented by an informal measure of linguistic security (Gal 1979), asking the informants to rate their knowledge of Czech and English on a one-to-five scale. In designing this questionnaire, I drew also on Dorian (1981), Gal (1979), Henzl (1975ms), and Pons (1990ms).

(3) Structured Linguistic Tasks and Elicited Narration. In addition to the naturalistic data and the questionnaire data, the analysis of my informants' performance on structured linguistic tasks has helped me identify semi-speakers (Dorian 1982; Schmidt 1985), and assess their proficiency in *TxCz*. I used the 100-word *lexicostatistic list* (Swadesh 1972); picture cards testing the speakers' ability to combine a *number+color+object* in the correctly declined form; the *sentence translation task* (twenty-five sentences) from English to Czech, focused on Moravian dialectical features; another *sentence translation task* (twenty sentences) from English to Czech, targeting the features of reduced Czech; and the *acceptability judgment task* (fifteen sentences), tapping their receptive competence in Czech. The dialectal task, together with naturally occurring speech, will afford a comparison of my findings with published research on historical Moravian dialects in Texas (Hannan 1992; Mendl 1976; Perkowski 1976). Informants' accounts of their use of Czech and their first encounters with English either at home or in school, usually narrated in both Czech and English, provide a comparable set of data to document both intra- and inter-speaker variability.

III. B. Historical Methods. Dr. Jakobson, an expert in Moravian ethnography, did seminal work in *TxCz* communities that spurred the interest in ethnic identity among Texas Czechs in the 1980s. Her collection of tapes will be used to examine the earlier stage of *TxCz* and map the progress of language shift to English as a primary language. I have provided the Center for American History in Austin, which holds this archive, with the scripts or full transcripts of about 150 tapes to serve as its initial catalogue (May 20– June 19, 1997). Much more work needs to be done before the whole collection becomes fully accessible to public.

III. C. Informants. In my search for informants I benefited from already established contacts with eighteen third-generation speakers in West (attending Westfest in the summer of 1996), with researchers who have worked on *TxCz*, and with advocates of Czech studies in Texas. During my stay in Austin, I sought urban speakers who had moved to the city from Granger or West. I used the methods of data collection outlined in (III.A) with eighty-five Granger and West informants (ranging in age from forty-six to ninety-five in Granger, and from thirty-six to eighty-seven in West), and conducted twenty-eight additional interviews in other Texas–Czech communities. While visiting these locales, I talked to many more community members, and distributed question-naires.

III. D. Transcription and Data Analysis. I recorded 327 hours of speech data and collected 270 attitudinal questionnaires. My transcriptions are selective, depending on the nature of data and the quality of tapes. In interviews, I focus on the central question of my inquiry, that is, *the role that an obsolescent language continues to play in the immigrant community and in the shifting definitions of its members' ethnic identity,* the issues of discontinued language transmission, and attitudes to the attempts for language revival. Other topics of interest are discussed above (III.A.1.). The data that I have already transcribed (i.e., interviews along with structured language tasks from thirty-nine focal informants from Granger and West), supplemented by field notes and these informants' questionnaires (III.A.2.), are the basis of my dissertation project (in-progress). Structured tasks (III.A.3.) were fully transcribed for the analysis of intra- and inter-speaker variability and types of dialectal features. The substance of naturally occurring speech will decide for the full or subset transcription of the remainder of the database. Although my primary interest is the content of both spontaneous and interview data, close attention to form, particularly in language tasks, has been instrumental in constructing accurate proficiency profiles of my Texan-Czech informants. At the next stage of this project I will use the Jakobson audio-tape collection (III.B.) as a comparative database.

III. E. Timetable. I began in Austin, cataloguing the Jakobson archive and searching for comparative data in her collection, as well as conducting my own interviews (5/20– 7/19). In mid-July, I moved to West, my first focal community (7/20–9/27), and then to Granger (9/28-11/26). While in West, I also visited Temple, Caldwell, Frenstat, New Tabor, and Ennis, to collect more data, distribute questionnaires, and conduct library research. During my stay in Granger, I extended my study to the nearby town of Taylor (namely the SPJST home for the elderly) and Corn Hill. Following my stay in Granger, I spent about two weeks traveling in the La Grange area (Fayetteville, Ellinger, Ammansville) and to the small communities surrounding Flatonia and Schulenburg (Dubina, Engle, Praha, Moravia, Novohrad, and Komensky), as well as to Shiner and Hallettsville.

IV. Research Significance

This project emphasizes the importance of an ethnographic, descriptive approach to the study of contexts of language use among *TxCz* speakers. It aims to identify the symbolic meanings of Czech ethnicity and of the Czech language in Texas, with the subsequent consequences for language survival. The ethnolinguistic perspective of this study will contribute to our understanding of how community members *themselves* perceive and assess the place of a reduced, dying language in the ethnic immigrant community, and provide insight into their reasoning about discontinued intergenerational language transmission and the nature of Czech "speakers."

Specifically, the study will contribute another local definition of a speech community affected by the language shift leading to language death, and show to what extent self-definitions of remaining *TxCz* speakers, as well as those of English monolinguals of Czech descent, still reflect the Moravian identity which was emphasized particularly by the first, and still is by the third, generation. It will show what role Czech remains to play in the speakers' identities, and what implications their attitudes have for the theories of language shift and attempts at language revival.

Further, this research will contribute to the body of data on immigrant languages in the United States where their situation has not been viewed with the same urgency as that of many indigenous languages approaching extinction (Hale 1992); after all, these reduced language varieties (Polinsky 1995) can be always compared with their healthy versions. Furthermore, the existing studies have traditionally aimed for structural description of language change, rather than the ethnolinguistic perspective that I assume in this project. I am concerned with more than language structure, viewing the community as a culturally constructed setting, populated by real speakers whose speech is of interest for both content and form. Thus by its focus and theoretical framework, this study should broaden the scope of research on "transplanted" (Eckert 1990) Slavic languages beyond the descriptive analysis of linguistic variation among immigrant speakers (e.g., Gilbert ed. 1970; Hammerová & Ripka 1994, on American Slovak; Polinsky, to appear, on American Russian; Rappaport 1990, on Texan Polish; Šabec 1995 on American Slovene). Furthermore, my data should add to the comparative research on ethnic Czechs in other *AmCz* communities, in Canada (e.g., Bubenik 1993), and Europe (cf. Eckert ed. 1993).

The significance of this project lies also in the opportunity to preserve and decode rare material existing only in one original set of audio-tapes and field notes which represent the two decades of Svatava Jakobson's data collection (1968-1985) on Texan Czech, providing yet another rich source of documentation for the communities' historical recontextualization.

References:

Appel, R. & Muysken, P. (1987). *Language contact and bilingualism.* London: Edward Arnold.

Bank, M. (1996). *Ethnicity: anthropological constructions.* New York: Routledge.

Banks, J. A. & Gay, G. (1978). Ethnicity in contemporary American society: Toward the development of typology. *Ethnicity,* 5. 238-251.

Barkan, E. R. (1995). Race, religion, and nationality in American society: A model of ethnicity from contact to assimilation. *Journal of American Ethnic History,* 14(2). 38-75.

Brenzinger, M. & Dimmendaal, G. J. (1992). Social contexts of language death. In M. Brenzinger (Ed.), *Language death. Factual and theoretical explorations with special reference to East Africa* (pp. 1-5). Berlin/New York: Mouton de Gruyter.

Bubenik, V. 1993. On the acquisition and maintenance of a minority language: Czech in Canada. In E. Eckert, (Ed.),s *Varieties of Czech* (pp. 241-253). Atlanta, GA: Rodopi.

Campbell, L. & Muntzel, M. C. (1989). The structural consequences of language death. In N. C. Dorian (Ed.), *Investigating obsolescence. Studies in language contraction and death* (pp. 81-196). Cambridge: Cambridge University Press.

Corder, S. P. (1973). *Introducing applied linguistics.* Harmondsworth: Penguin.

The Czech Texans (1972). San Antonio, TX: The Institute of Texas Cultures.

Denison, N. (1977). Language death or language suicide? *International Journal of the Sociology of Language,* 12. 13-22.

Dopke, S. (1986). Discourse structures in bilingual families. *Journal of Multilingual and Multicultural Development* 7(6), 493-505.

Dorian, N. C. (1977). The problem of the semi-speaker in language death. *International Journal of the Sociology of Language,* 12. 23-32.

_____ (1981). *Language death: the life cycle of a Scottish Gaelic dialect.* Philadelphia: U of Pennsylvania Press.

_____ (1982). Defining the speech community to include its working margins. In S. Romaine (Ed.), *Sociolinguistic variation in speech communities* (pp. 25-33). London: Edward Arnold.

_____ (1986). Abrupt transmission failure in obsolescing languages: How sudden the "tip" to the dominant language in communities and families?. In V. Nikiforidu, M. Van Clay, M. Niepokuj & D. Feder (Eds.), *Proceedings of the twelfth annual meeting of the Berkeley Linguistic Society.* Berkeley, CA: Berkeley Linguistics Society.

_____ (Ed.). (1989). *Investigating obsolescence. Studies in language contraction and death.* Cambridge: Cambridge University Press.

_____ (1995). Small languages and small language communities. *International Journal of Sociology of Language*, 114. 129-137.

Dressler, W. U. (1981). Language shift and language death—a protean challenge for the linguist. *Folia Linguistica*, 15(1-2). 5-28.

Eckert, E. (1987). Lexicon of the first generation American Czechs. *Review of Applied Linguistics*, 76. 25-41.

_____ (1988). First-generation American Czech: A sociolinguistic survey. *Language Problems and Language Planning*, 12(2). 97-109.

_____ (1990). Simplification in transplanted languages: a study of motion verbs in American Czech. *Review of Applied Linguistics*, 87-88. 95-118.

_____ (1993). *Varieties of Czech. Studies in sociolinguistics.* Atlanta: Rodopi.

Fantini, A. (1985). *Language acquisition of a bilingual child. A sociolinguistic perspective.* Clevedon: Multilingual Matters.

Fishman, J. A. et al. (Eds.). (1966). *Language loyalty in the United States.* London/The Hague: Mouton.

Fishman, J. A. (1989). *Language and ethnicity in minority sociolinguistic perspective.* Philadelphia: Multilingual Matters.

_____ (1991a). *Reversing language shift.* Philadelphia: Multilingual Matters, LTD, 76.

_____ (1991b). *Yiddish: Turning to life.* Amsterdam/Philadelphia: John Benjamins.

Gal, S. (1979). *Language shift: Social determinants of linguistic change in bilingual Austria.* NY: Academic Press.

Gilbert, G. G. (Ed.). (1970). *Texas studies in bilingualism: Spanish, French, German, Czech, Polish, Sorbian, and Norwegian in the Southwest.* Berlin: Walter de Gruyter & Co.

Gudykunst, W. B. (Ed.). 1988. *Language and ethnic identity.* Cleveland: Multilingual Matters.

Gumperz, J. (1982). *Discourse strategies.* Cambridge, England: Cambridge University Press.

_____ (1986). The speech community. In P. P. Giglioli (Ed.), *Language and social context* (2nd ed., pp. 219-231). New York: Penguin Books.

Haarmann, H. (1986). *Language in ethnicity.* New York: Mouton de Gruyter.

Hale, K. et al. (1992). Endangered languages. *Language*, 68(1). 1-42.

Hammerova, L. & Ripka, I. (1994). *Speech of American Slovaks.* Bratislava: Veda.

Hanak, M. (1979). Reformist tradition and courage to synthesis: the Czech experiment in democratic justice. In C. Machann (Ed.), *The Czechs in Texas: a symposium* (pp. 173-183). College Station, TX: Texas A&M University.

Hannan, K. (1985). *A study of the culture of the Czech-Moravian community of Texas.* Unpublished manuscript.

_____ (1996a). Ethnic identity among the Czechs and Moravians of Texas. *Journal of American Ethnic History* 15(4). 3-31.

_____ (1996b). *Borders of language and identity in Teschen Silesia.* New York: Peter Lang Publishing.

Haugen, E. (1969). *The Norwegian language in America. A study in bilingual behavior.* Bloomington: Indiana UP.

Henzl, V. M. (1975). *Cultivation and maintenance of literary Czech by American speakers.* Unpublished doctoral dissertation, Stanford University.

_____ (1981). Slavic languages in the new environment. In C. A. Ferguson & S. B. Heath (Eds.), *Language in the USA* (pp. 293-321). New York: Cambridge University Press.

Hewitt, W. P. (1978). *The Czechs in Texas: A Study of the immigration and the development of Czech ethnicity 1850-1920.* Unpublished doctoral dissertation, University of Texas at Austin.

Hill, J. H. (1979). Language death, language contact, and language evolution. In S. A. Wurm & W. M. Cormack (Eds.), *Approaches to language* (pp. 45-78). The Hague: Mouton & Company.

_____ (1983). Language death in Uto-Aztecan. *International Journal of American Linguistics,* 49. 258-276.

_____ (1993). Structure and practice in language shift. In K. Hyltenstam & A. Viberg (Eds.), *Progression and regression in language* (pp. 68-93). Cambridge, England: Cambridge University Press.

Hill, J. H. & Hill, K (1986). *Speaking Mexicano. Dynamics of syncretic language in Central Mexico.* Tucson: The University of Arizona Press.

Hymes, D. (1974). *Foundations in sociolinguistics. An ethnographic approach.* Philadelphia: University of Pennsylvania Press.

Krauss, M. (1992). The world's languages in crisis. *Language 68*(1), 4-13.

Kučera, K. (1989).*Český jazyk v USA. (Czech language in the USA).* Praha: Universita Karlová.

Kulick, D. (1992). *Language shift and cultural reproduction.* Cambridge, England: Cambridge University Press.

Kutac, M. M. (1967). *English loanwords in the Czech literary language of Texas.* Unpublished M.A. thesis, University of Texas at Austin.

Labov, W. (1972). *Sociolinguistic patterns.* Philadelphia: University of Pennsylvania Press.

Machalek, R. (1979). The ambivalence of ethnoreligion. In C. Machann (Ed.), *The Czechs in Texas: A symposium* (pp. 95-114).

Machann, C. (1976). The current state of the Czech language in Texas. In B. Hoffer & B. L. Dubois (Eds.), *Southwest areal linguistics then and now. Proceedings of the Fifth Southwest Areal Language and Linguistic Workshop* (pp. 270-279). Trinity University.

Machann, C. (Ed.). (1979). *Papers from 'The Czechs in Texas: A symposium'.* College Station, TX: Texas A&M University Press.

Machann, C. & Mendl, J. W. (1983). *Krásná Amerika: A study of the Texas Czechs, 1851-1939.* Austin, TX: Eakin Press.

Maresh, H. R. (1946). The Czechs in Texas. *The Southwest Historical Quarterly L,* 336-240.

Maresh, H. R. & Hudson, E. (1934, reprint. 1996). *Czech pioneers of the Southwest.* Houston: Western Lithograph.

Mendl, J. W. (1976). *Texas Czech: Historical Czech dialects in the New World.* Unpublished M.A. thesis, University of Texas at Austin.

Ochs, E. (1988). *Culture and language development.* Cambridge: Cambridge University Press.

Olesch, R. (1970). The West Slavic languages in Texas with special regard to Sorbian in Serbin, Lee County. In G. G. Gilbert (Ed.), *Texas studies in bilingualism* (pp. 150-169).

Papademetre, L. (1994). Self-defined, other defined cultural identity: Logogenesis and multiple-group membership in a Greek Australian sociolinguistic community. *Journal of Multilingual and Multicultural Development 14*(4), 275-286.

Perkowski, J. (1976). Linguistic change in Texas Czech. In M. Rechcígl, Jr. (Ed.), *Studies in Czechoslovak history II* (pp. 148-153). Meerut, India: Sadhna Prakashan.

Polasek, T. (1979). Early life in Moravia, Texas. In C. Machann (Ed.), *The Czechs in Texas: a symposium* (pp. 142-147).

Polinsky, M. (1995). Cross-linguistic parallels in language loss. *Southwest Journal of Linguistics* 14 (1). 87-123.

Pons, C. R. (1990). *Language death among Waldesians of Valdese.* Unpublished Ph.D. dissertation, Indiana University.

Rappaport, G. C. (1990). "The linguistic situation of Americans of Polish descent in Texas." In W. Miudenka (ed.), *Jezyk polski w swiecie* (pp. 159-178). Cracow: PWN.

Romaine, S. (Ed.). (1982). *Sociolinguistic variation in speech communities.* London: Edward Arnold.

Sasse, H. J. (1992a). Theory of language death. In Brenzinger, M. (Ed.), *Language death* (pp. 7-30).

_____ (1992b). Language decay and contact-induced change: similarities and differences. In M. Brenzinger (Ed.), *Language death* (pp. 59-80).

Schieffelin, B. B. & Ochs, E. (1986). *Language socialization across cultures.* Cambridge: Cambridge University Press.

Schieffelin, B. B. (1990). *The give and take of everyday life. Language socialization of Kaluli children.* Cambridge: Cambridge University Press.

Schmidt, A. (1985). *Young people's Dyirbal: An example of language death from Australia.* Cambridge, England: Cambridge University Press.

Silva-Corvalan, C. (1994). *Language contact and change: Spanish in Los Angeles.* Oxford: Clarendon.

Skrabanek, R. (1988). *We're Czechs.* College Station, TX: Texas A&M University Press.

Smith, C. S. (1991). *The demise of Czech in two Texas communities.* Unpublished doctoral dissertation, The University of Texas at Austin.

Splawn, V. M. (1972). *Sociological study of a Czech community in Ellis County, Texas.* Unpublished M.A. thesis, University of Texas at Austin.

Stasney, M. E. (1938). *The Czechs in Texas.* Unpublished M.A. thesis, University of Texas at Austin.

Swadesh, M. (1972). *The origin and diversification of language.* Chicago/New York: Aldine/Atherton.

Weinreich, U. (1968). *Languages in contact: Findings and problems.* The Hague/Paris: Mouton.

Woolard, K. A. (1989). Language convergence and language death as social processes. In N. C. Dorian (ed.), *Investigating obsolescence* (pp. 355-367).

Toward a Biography of
Thomas Čapek (1861–1950):

Sources, Life Sketch, and
Biographical Models

David Zdeněk Chroust

Introduction

In the 1990s, several biographical monographs have appeared in the field of Czech-American historiography. Machann and Mendl (1991) selected, translated, and annotated several of the biographical articles that were a regular feature of the Chicago almanac *Amerikán* throughout its eighty-year existence from 1877 to 1957. Other scholars published original studies of outstanding individual Czech-Americans. Chrislock (1993) wrote about Charles Jonas, a leading Czech-American journalist who made a distinguished career in Wisconsin politics and in the American consular service. Šolle (1994) focused on Vojta Náprstek, who provided leadership to the incipient Czech community as a journalist and organizer during his ten-year sojourn in America, and who built the museum that bears his name after his return to Prague in 1858.[29]

Náprstek, Jonas, and the individuals portrayed in the Machann and Mendl volume, all belong to the initial period of Czech-American history, which commenced with the arrival of the first immigrants in the late 1840s and is traditionally extended to the successful conclusion of the Czechoslovak independence movement at the end of the First World War. This was a "golden age" of vibrant Czech language cultural life and self-sufficient enclaves in America's cities and rural districts. (The term "mass immigration" has also been used as a label for this period, but it is misleading, since Czechs began arriving en masse only well after the Civil War, and the influx lasted only until the outbreak of war in 1914.) It is to be hoped that scholars on both sides of the Atlantic will build on the excellent beginning made in the 1990s in biographical scholarship on the "golden age" of Czech-America.

One important figure who deserves a separate monograph is Thomas Čapek (1861-1950), an attorney and banker who published some twenty English and Czech language books and pamphlets on the Czechs in America. Čapek was the most prolific of the writers who described this American ethnic group. *The Čechs (Bohemians) in America*, which he published in 1920, is still the only general survey in English, although it was outclassed by a far more extensive and encyclopedic Czech-language edition that Čapek published six years later in Prague, *Naše Amerika* (Our America). As a bibliographer, Čapek published a volume on the Czech-American periodical press (1911) and another, with his wife, Anna Čapková, née Vostrovská (1867-1956), on English-language Bohemica (1918). As a publicist for Czech and Slovak interests, Čapek published *The Slovaks of Hungary* (1906) and *Bohemia under Hapsburg Misrule* (1915). Besides being the author of these and numerous minor publications, Čapek was an important Czech-American for several other reasons: as editor of Czech-American periodicals, as a public figure active in various organizations and undertakings on behalf of Czech-Americans and Czechoslovakia, as president of the Bank of Europe in New York, and as a personal acquaintance or correspondent of most of the outstanding Czech-Americans of his time.[30]

Sources

Despite Čapek's importance, little has been written about him. In 1911, Čeněk Zíbrt (1864-1932), a librarian at the Czech National Museum in Prague, published a lengthy article in the museum's journal reviewing books about the Czechs in America recently published by Jan Habenicht (1840-1917), Jaroslav Egon Salaba Vojan (1872-1944), and Thomas Čapek. Although Zíbrt became acquainted with Čapek during the American's first return trip to Bohemia in 1903, Zíbrt included no biographical details in his article. The first biographical article about Čapek appeared in 1926 in the journal *Naše zahraničí* (Our Communities Abroad) on the occasion of Čapek's sixty-fifth birthday, but this was merely a brief sketch in the style of an encyclopedia entry. Twenty years later, the journal of the Czechoslovak Genealogical Society published a similar commemorative article, reprinted as a pamphlet in 1947. In America, the only substantive article can be found in the 1933 volume of the almanac *Amerikán.* Although only four pages long, this article not only recounts the most important facts of Čapek's life but also provides some revealing details. The author, Jaroslav E. S. Vojan, was a personal friend of Čapek's and, like Čapek, an attorney and author of books about the Czech immigrants.[31]

Čapek published a memoir, *Moje Amerika* (My America), in Prague in 1935. Subtitled *Vzpomínky a úvahy* (Memories and Thoughts), this work serves as a reminder of the fact, often forgotten, that the genre of the memoir stands distinct from that of the autobiography. *Moje Amerika* is not an autobiography: Čapek devotes as much space—perhaps more—to his many acquaintances as to himself. When he turns to his life, his account is uneven, discussing some periods at length, such as his childhood and youth in Bohemia and his activities during World War I, while glossing over others, such as the years after he returned to New York as a husband and father in 1895. Also evident in *Moje Amerika* is a bias in favor of the extraordinary over the everyday. For example, Čapek devotes seventeen pages to his 1903 trip to Bohemia and tour of the Balkans, where dramatic political events were unfolding. By contrast, he leaves the story of the law office he operated on Manhattan's E. 72nd Street largely untold, even after he arouses the reader's interest and expectations with two tantalizing statements: "those eleven years [1899-1910] I count among the happiest in my life," and "few Czechs arriving in New York failed to drop in." Another limitation of *Moje Amerika* is inherent in its date of publication: the last major event in this narrative is the liquidation of the Bank of Europe, of which Čapek was president, in August 1931, yet two more decades remained in Čapek's life. *Moje Amerika* is one of the most important sources on which any future biography of Čapek must draw, but it is no substitute for such a biography.[32]

Of Thomas Čapek's other publications, two figure as sources useful in the study of his life: *Jan Vratislav Čapek* and *Z New Yorku do Prahy a zpět* (From New York to Prague and Back). Jan Vratislav Čapek (1842-1909) was the first of the four Čapek brothers to emigrate to America. This pamphlet biography sheds much light on Thomas Čapek's family, the early influences that shaped him, and the circumstances behind his emigration to America. *Z New Yorku do Prahy a zpět* is a collection of letters Čapek wrote to his wife, Anna, documenting his trip to the new state of Czechoslovakia in the fall of 1921.[33]

Čapek also documented his life in the manuscript material that he produced and collected. As deposited in the Library of Congress in the years after his death by his widow, the collection contains some six thousand items. By far the largest part of the Čapek Papers consists of sources he gathered for use in his publications about Czech-America. Still, the much smaller section devoted to biographical material about Čapek, his wife, and son Thomas Jr. (1895-1987) contains valuable correspondence, other manuscripts, memorabilia, and newspaper clippings. Elsewhere in the collection is a class of materials that can also be used as biographical sources: issues of several Czech-American periodicals with which Čapek and his brother Jan Vratislav were associated. Runs range from a single issue of *New Yorské humoristické listy* (New York Humorous Leaves) (1887) to an apparently complete file of *Patriot* (New York, 1883-1884). Even the source material that Čapek used to write his books could probably be profitably culled for biographical information, especially the voluminous correspondence from Čapek's informants.

The ample and varied array of primary source material that Čapek left behind about himself brings up the problem of balance. Modern biography recognizes the dangers in relying too heavily on sources produced by the subject and attempts to draw in equal measure on the testimony of other informants. The dearth of secondary sources on Čapek has already been described.

Unfortunately, primary source material written by Čapek's

acquaintances and associates is equally hard to come by. The first reason, as Čapek laments in his books, is that his contemporaries in the Czech-American community gave scant thought to the value of their personal papers and of the archives of organizations in which they were active. As a result, little of this material has survived. Čapek's own papers are a shining exception.

The second reason is that some of the people who knew Čapek best were private, ordinary citizens whose records are rarely preserved. Even biographers of far more prominent subjects encounter this problem. When the subject is someone of only modest prominence, like Čapek, the problem tends to be more difficult. In *Moje Amerika*, Čapek mentions numerous people with whom he had close relations during various periods in his life. For example, in the chapter on his second Omaha period, 1890-1894, where he launched his law practice, Čapek mentions exchanging daily visits with three fellow attorneys from another law office. References to debates about capitalism and to impassioned singing during these daily visits mark the attorneys as promising informants. But, even if they recorded their impressions of Čapek, it is doubtful that the papers of these obscure attorneys could still be found. Curiously, Čapek fails to mention even one of his business associates at the Bank of Europe by name in his memoir. Čapek was president of the bank and spent the longest and final period of his career there, from 1910 to 1931. No testimony about Čapek, however, can be expected from these reticent, self-effacing bankers. In fact, after Čapek published *Bohemia under Hapsburg Misrule*, the board of directors expressed displeasure that he was mixing writing with banking: "I was politely made to understand that I should stick to banking." On the other hand, the views of some of Čapek's acquaintances who were equally obscure were recorded and preserved. Václav Alois Jung (1858-1927) was a minor writer and journalist whom Čapek befriended in Omaha. When Čapek criticized his writings, Jung published two reports that Čapek found "aggressive" retorts in *Směr* (Direction), a newspaper in Plzeň, Bohemia.[34]

Not all of Čapek's acquaintances were obscure. His first employer in Omaha, Jan Rosický (1845-1910), editor of *Pokrok západu* (Progress of the West), was one of the most prominent Czech-Americans of his time. Čapek's friendship with Theodore

Roosevelt began in 1895, when the latter was police commissioner of New York. As an attorney, Čapek sued William Vanderbilt on behalf of a Czech immigrant who had lost two fingers while working on the tycoon's estate. During his brief political career in the Nebraska legislature, Čapek was associated with William Jennings Bryan and later corresponded with him. Čapek was on intimate terms with Thomas Masaryk and spent a part of his 1921 visit to Czechoslovakia as a guest at the presidential estate in Lány. It remains to be seen if the papers of these great historical figures have anything to say about Čapek.[35]

Another category of informants integral to biography are descendants of the subject and of his relatives. These informants are potential sources of anecdotes and stories that are part of the orally transmitted family lore and may describe revealing life events, personal circumstances, and character traits that were unknown to or unnoticed by other sources. Descendants and relatives may also possess personal papers, photographs, personal effects, and memorabilia that shed light on the subject or once belonged to him. The number of such items likely to be found among a subject's descendants and relatives naturally declines with the passage of time since the subject's death, as does the number, detail, and reliability of stories about him in family lore. With the passage of time, living descendants and relatives also become more difficult to identify and locate. For these reasons, the biographer must consider the length of time that has elapsed since a subject's death as he plans his research and evaluates the potential role of living descendants and relatives as sources.

At twenty-five to thirty years between generations, Thomas Čapek was born five generations ago. Nevertheless, his descendants and relatives are still worth pursuing as informants. First, the family into which Čapek was born was large, and so was his cohesive extended family. Čapek had four brothers, two sisters, three paternal uncles, two paternal aunts, and four maternal aunts. Living descendants of Čapek's siblings and cousins are apt to be numerous. (By contrast, Čapek's wife had just one brother and one sister. Also, Anna Čapková was far removed from her extended family in the Czech lands. Unlike her husband, Anna Čapková was born in the United States of immigrant parents.) Secondly, Čapek exhibited a lifelong interest in his relatives. His emotional attachment to them was strong, and he knew even distant relatives from personal contact, which makes their descendants promising informants. Most of Čapek's extended family lived in his native Chráštovice and in nearby villages in the Strakonice district of southern Bohemia. Visits by various relatives were a regular occurrence in Čapek's childhood home, as he relates in *Moje Amerika*, and he remained in this native region, enmeshed in a cohesive extended family, throughout his formative years. Even after his emigration to America, Čapek maintained his ties with relatives. Besides three brothers, he had two cousins in the New World, Josef and František Hrouda of Cleveland, sons of a maternal aunt. A niece, May Čapková, was a permanent member of the Čapek household after her father, Jan Vratislav Čapek, died. The energy and devotion Čapek brought to maintaining family ties is suggested by a passage in *Moje Amerika* about how he discovered a great-granddaughter of a paternal aunt among the depositors of his New York bank! (We can imagine Čapek's dismay when the skeptical young woman refused to believe his detailed account of how they were related.) Čapek also renewed ties with relatives in the Czech lands during his visits there in 1903, 1921, 1923, 1926, 1928, and 1935.[36]

Finally, living descendants of Čapek's relatives are still worth pursuing as informants because Čapek's writings make the task of finding them easier. The forty-seven relatives listed in the personal name index to *Moje Amerika* are identified by full name and relationship to Thomas Čapek, while the corresponding passages often give place of residence, occupation, names of children, and other personal details. In some cases, *Moje Amerika* even provides references to obituaries. References to the obituaries published in four Czech-American newspapers after the deaths of Čapek's brother Ladislav Matěj Čapek (1847-1925) and his wife Kateřina, *née* Landová, (died 1933) are convenient starting points for an attempt to discover the fate and possible descendants of their daughter, Lada. The Internet is a dazzling new research tool that can be used to capitalize on the many "leads" in Čapek's writings with amazing speed and ease. Just one day after this author posted a message to *Knihovna,* a listserve in the Czech Republic for librarians, he received several well-informed responses by e-mail with advice on how to do biographical research in the Czech

Republic, where to find information about those Čapeks who remained in Bohemia, and about their living descendants. One respondent provided the Strakonice address and telephone number of a direct descendant of Čapek's brother Václav and even offered to print and mail e-mail queries to this descendant as a means of accelerating the research process. As a further surprise, this respondent enlisted the help of her husband, a descendant of Čapek's sister Anna Slanařová, in tracing another branch of the Čapek family.[37]

It remains to be seen whether these living descendants, so many generations removed from Thomas Čapek, have anything new and substantive to say about him and whether searching for other living descendants would be a worthwhile effort. As weak as the grounds for optimism might appear, Čapek's only direct descendant, granddaughter Ludmila Leong, far exceeded reasonable expectations and turned out to be an extremely helpful and resourceful informant. From 1944, Leong, her parents, and her paternal grandparents, Thomas and Anna Čapek, lived in the same New York apartment building. In a well-written letter to the author, Leong described many details of her grandfather's last six years. *The Čapek Papers* at the Library of Congress are probably the only other source that might shed light on the final period of his life. Regardless, however, of what may eventually be found there, this collection is complete as it stands. By contrast, Leong's recollections are a body of source material in the making, to be developed in further letters and interviews. In addition, she possesses manuscript material that did not find its way into the Čapek Papers. In her letter, she enclosed prints of fourteen portraits and quoted from the diary that her grandmother kept during the 1893 World's Fair in Chicago, where Anna and Thomas Čapek met and courted.[38]

Life Sketch

Thomas Čapek was born on December 6, 1861, as the seventh and last child of a peasant family in Chráštovice. Both the family and the rural district in which it had been rooted for generations were Czech. In the year before Čapek's birth, a constitution was promulgated in Vienna, and a parliament formed. These momentous changes brought a period of stifling absolutism to an end and inaugurated a new era in the Habsburg Empire. Under these new circumstances, the Czech nation developed its cultural and economic life with great energy in the decades that followed and also became increasingly assertive in the political arena. Their ambition to reclaim preeminence in the culture, economy, and government of their home provinces brought the Czechs into conflict with the Germans, who formed a large minority in Bohemia and Moravia, where many districts, especially on the periphery, were inhabited almost exclusively by Germans. Čapek grew up in this heady atmosphere of national renaissance and ethnic conflict. It was an atmosphere that nurtured devotion and service to one's nation—values evident in Čapek's life work as a researcher and author.

A remarkable series of national successes and setbacks electrified and stunned Czech society during the years of Čapek's childhood and youth. The 1867 compromise reorganized the empire in the interests of the Germans and Hungarians but ignored the Czechs, who, like the Hungarians, also had a lapsed kingdom to resurrect and "historic rights" to restore. The surly, defiant mood in the Czech areas of Bohemia and Moravia turned to elation in 1871 when the Hohenwart cabinet and Emperor Franz Joseph in Vienna prepared to accede to Czech demands for autonomy. Bitter disappointment followed when the Emperor drew back, Hohenwart resigned, and a severe military governor was dispatched to Bohemia. Demonstrations of national resolve and vitality, as well as Pan-Slavic solidarity, were a favorite means of responding to such setbacks. In the year of the Austro-Hungarian compromise, a large and outspoken Czech delegation traveled to Moscow for a Pan-Slavic Congress. The movement to build the National Theater in Prague mobilized and stirred the nation with its appeal to national pride, reliance on donations from the masses, and use of building material from around the country. Monuments to national heroes were built, such as the one to Josef Jungmann in Prague in 1873, and their unveiling became the occasion for jubilant mass rallies. The 1870s were also a time of rift and profound debate on the Czech political scene as the Young Czech Party emerged and, with its emphasis on assertiveness over deference in

Czech relations with the Habsburg and German establishment, challenged the authority and policies of the Old Czechs, led by František Palacký and František Ladislav Rieger.

Chráštovice was remote from Prague and other centers of national life, as well as from the ethnically mixed districts where the struggle between Czechs and Germans for dominance in Bohemia was most visible. But Bohemia was a small, developed, and literate province, and during this era of nationalism, news of important events and issues, as well as intellectual currents, penetrated the countryside. Passages in Čapek's writings suggest that Czech nationalism and the Czech-German conflict exerted influence on his development. For example, Čapek recalled witnessing his father denounced as an inveterate political debater in the village pub. As a messenger for his mother, Čapek was a frequent visitor to the pub. Čapek probably also heard about Czech national affairs from secondary school and university students. Students were among the most nationally conscious segments of Czech society, and Jan Vratislav Čapek was enrolled at the university in Prague from 1864 to 1871. For a part of this period, he also worked as a clerk for František Švestka, an attorney and a representative in the Bohemian provincial legislature. Thomas Čapek seldom saw Jan Vratislav Čapek, but two other elder brothers, Ladislav Matěj Čapek and Josef Valerián Čapek (born 1849), attended secondary school, and the family house in Chráštovice frequently hosted numerous other students: cousins, neighbors, and schoolmates of the Čapek brothers.[39]

By 1873, when he was sent to Písek to attend the town *reálka*, a secondary school, Thomas Čapek apparently had a well-developed Czech identity. In Písek he attended the Czech theater, and after one performance, he and other enthusiastic students accompanied the leading actress to her hotel suite. The theater was an established and effective means of inspiring and spreading national consciousness among the Czechs. Čapek studied in Písek for three years. The very choice of a Czech *reálka* was revealing, because German secondary schools were also nearby, and some Czech students attended them, including Čapek's brother Jan Vratislav Čapek, who spent four years at the *Kreis-Hauptschule* in Klatovy before moving on to the Czech school in Písek. Thomas Čapek's first experiences in a German environment came at a later age. From Písek he went to Strakonice as a sales apprentice in the Fürth firm, a German manufacturer of fezzes. By now, Čapek's Czech identity was firmly established: in his memoirs, he wrote with unconcealed resentment about the Germanizing character of both workplace and town.[40]

The entrenched German element that offended Čapek's Czech sensibilities was not the only reason for his unhappiness in Strakonice: he was a sales apprentice not by his own choice, and his duties and prospects as a sales apprentice did not appeal to him. Čapek wanted to continue his education and considered entering one of several professions. He was an avid reader and a serious student. Čapek's father, Jan (1814-1870), had memories of serfdom and wanted to give his sons the means to avoid the hard life of the peasant by providing for their education. Unfortunately, Jan did not have the financial means to realize his plans for his sons. Jan Vratislav Čapek was an inspiring role model for his younger brothers, but he was also the only beneficiary of his father's plans, and even he could not finish his university studies for lack of funds. By the time Thomas Čapek was in the midst of his secondary school years, his father was dead, and Jan Vratislav Čapek was in America. Presumably, his brother Václav, who had inherited the family farm, vetoed Thomas' plans and made the decision to send him to Strakonice.

Čapek describes his sales apprenticeship as "three wasted years" and devotes barely two pages of his memoirs to this period of "painful disappointment." From Strakonice, Čapek emigrated to America. He does not discuss his reasons for emigrating, but frustration and the desire to continue his education certainly accounted for much of his motivation. Other likely factors were the desire to avoid military service and the lure and romance of America. In 1870 the Čapek family had strained to obtain the cash required to "buy" Václav out of the obligatory years of service in the Austrian army. Thomas had no such prospect. No doubt, the fact that he was approaching military age and might be detained at the border was on his mind, because he traveled on a borrowed passport.[41]

The "push" of eventual army duty was matched by the "pull" of America. By the time of Čapek's youth, the image of America as an exotic paradise and El Dorado was well established in the

Czech imagination. For Čapek, America was not just an abstraction: three of his elder brothers were there. Jan Vratislav Čapek arrived in New York on August 18, 1871, and proceeded to Cleveland to take up the editorship of the Freethinker weekly *Pokrok* (Progress) (Chicago, September 25, 1867-Cleveland, August 8, 1878). A year earlier, Jan Vratislav Čapek had responded to an appeal in Prague's *Národní listy* (Nation's Pages) from Josef Václav Sýkora, a Cleveland notary and real estate agent, who had wanted to correspond with former classmates from the Písek *reálka*. After *Pokrok* editor František Zdrůbek resigned in the wake of a libel suit filed by Vilém J. Řepiš, priest of Cleveland's St. Václav parish, Sýkora nominated Čapek as Zdrůbek's replacement. Thomas Čapek became an avid reader of *Pokrok* and of the rival Cleveland weekly *Národní noviny* (National Newspaper) (October 2, 1873-September 3, 1874), which Jan Vratislav Čapek launched after his resignation from *Pokrok* on August 7, 1873. Two other Čapek brothers arrived in America in 1872, Josef Valerián Čapek in May and Ladislav Matěj Čapek in October. They collaborated with Jan Vratislav Čapek on *Národní noviny* and its predecessor, *Diblík* (Imp), launched on November 15, 1872. In Chráštovice, the Čapek brothers and their newspapers were well known. The villagers referred to Jan Vratislav Čapek as *pan doktor Johan*. Hearing this and recalling the poverty and desperation that his brother had suffered in Prague, Thomas Čapek may well have been impressed by the achievements that were possible in America and turned to thoughts of what he might make of himself there. The allure of America as an exotic land of adventure was also not lost on Thomas Čapek: a story about Indians published serially in one of the Cleveland newspapers fired his imagination.[42]

When Thomas Čapek arrived in the port of New York aboard the *Moselle* from Bremen in the second half of 1879, Jan Vratislav Čapek was waiting for him at the dock, and Čapek stayed in his brother's Brooklyn home for more than four years. During these first years in America, the two great themes of Čapek's life can already be recognized: the making of a "self-made man" and the work of an author in the service of his ethnic group. In America, Čapek responded both to the ethos of the country to which he had chosen to immigrate and to the ethos of the native land he left behind. America was the "land of opportunity," where immigrants of peasant origin were free of the limitations of class and could achieve wealth and a more prestigious "station" in life. Bohemia was the "outpost of Slavdom in a German sea," where the Czech nation had withstood calamities and resisted assimilation. This ethos inspired individuals to contribute to the work of affirming and developing the nation's perpetually threatened identity. Whereas the ethos of late nineteenth-century America was personified by the "captains of industry," like the Scottish immigrant Andrew Carnegie, the ethos of Bohemia was exemplified by the *buditelé národa*, "awakeners of the nation," like the historian František Palacký. In the life of Thomas Čapek, the ethos of America was expressed in his career as an attorney and banker, while the ethos of Bohemia found an outlet in his work as a journalist, community spokesman, and scholar.

The concept of the "self-made man" held a profound attraction for Čapek. He used the term repeatedly in his publications — even the Czech-language ones — to describe himself and other Czech immigrants who achieved affluence and prestige in American society. The preference for a familiar environment kept most immigrants in their ethnic enclaves and in constrained circumstances. To become a "self-made man" required seeking one's fortune, or at least part of it, in the broader, English speaking society. This was an unsettling, even frightening, prospect. Besides the skills, time, and effort required to enter a profession or launch a business, the immigrant "self-made man" had to master a foreign language and culture, and he had to contend with discrimination, ridicule, and hostility from many Americans. Where Čapek found the inspiration and determination to become a "self-made man" is one of the fundamental questions to be addressed in an eventual biography. Certainly, his childhood experiences were inspiration enough for the desire to escape poverty, while the value of education was an article of faith preached by his father. Additional inspiration may have come from Čapek's reading and from the example of individual Czech immigrants in America. For example, Josef Václav Sýkora, who had brought Jan Vratislav Čapek to America, transformed himself from shop clerk to owner of a real estate agency in Cleveland's central business district. Perhaps Sýkora served as the archetype of the "self-made man." However, even

Sýkora never mastered English and depended on the immigrant neighborhoods for clients.[43]

Čapek's ideal of the "self-made man," and his personal realization of it, began to take shape even as he was en route to America: "The thought that was on my mind day and night was to go to school in America and become an architect." Čapek was methodical in the way he went about the business of making a career in the professions and securing a respectable place for himself in American society. He realized that the first step toward this goal was to master the English language, and he devoted the first three years in New York to voracious reading and home study. Jan Vratislav Čapek's Brooklyn house became Thomas' "supplemental secondary school." Thomas Čapek also attended the theater and listened to public speakers ranging from Congregational minister Henry Ward Beecher to politicians at public rallies. The novels of Horatio Alger, who lived in New York, were popular in this period, and Čapek was probably familiar with them and their heroes: destitute youths like Čapek who relied on diligence, resourcefulness, and ambition to climb from a lowly occupation to the presidency of the company. Čapek was fortunate to have a brother who was willing and able to provide for his material needs while he devoted himself fully to studying the English language and American culture. A year before Thomas' arrival, Jan Vratislav Čapek married Luisa Schaefer, daughter of a prosperous baker from Germany.[44]

Thomas Čapek did not seek employment until January 1883, when he became a typesetter and reporter for *Dělnické listy* (Workingmen's Pages) (first published in Cleveland, May 22, 1875). After several months, however, this socialist newspaper ceased publication, being outcompeted by a rival and more radical competitor, *Dělník Americký* (American Worker) (October 10, 1882-August 9, 1886), founded by disgruntled typesetters who defected from *Dělnické listy*. On August 18, 1883, Jan Vratislav Čapek, Thomas Čapek, and František Bartošek, a greengrocer, published the first issue of *Patriot*. This weekly, which counseled against labor radicalism, consistently failed to make a profit, was attacked by *Dělník Americký*, and ceased publication in January 1884. A month later, Thomas Čapek went to Omaha, Nebraska, at the invitation of Jan Rosický, editor of *Pokrok západu* (August 1,

1871-December 29, 1920), and remained there as assistant editor until the end of June 1886. By then, he had made the decision to enroll at the University of Michigan in Ann Arbor and pursue a degree in law. It is hard to see how the uncertain prospects, long hours, and meager pay of a Czech-American journalist, especially in New York, could have diverted him permanently from resuming his education. What influenced him in Nebraska to choose law, however, is unclear. Perhaps it was the example of Louis Berka (1855-1930), the only Czech attorney in Omaha. Berka was also elected to terms as county judge and state legislator, and Čapek made a brief career in local and state politics after his return to Omaha. Unlike Josef Václav Sýkora of Cleveland, Berka was "more American than Czech, having come to America as a boy."[45]

At Michigan, Čapek earned a law degree in 1888. He took further courses at Columbia University in New York. But these courses were in literature and economics, and he left Columbia without earning a degree. Instead, he returned to Omaha in 1890 and opened a law practice in the building of the Omaha National Bank. After several months, lack of success compelled him to take a partner, Louis J. Piatti. Czech residents were their most numerous clients, but others were of French and Italian origin, the nationalities of Piatti's immigrant parents. Involvement in politics was a natural accompaniment to the practice of law, and it was all the more attractive for the presence of numerous Czechs in elected office. Edward Rosewater (1841-1906), owner of Omaha's Czech publishing house, *Národní tiskárna*, was a prominent leader of the Republican Party in Nebraska. In 1884-1886, as editor of *Pokrok západu*, which the Czech Jew had founded, Čapek "saw Rosewater daily." After his return to Omaha, Čapek also became acquainted with William Jennings Bryan, the Democratic Party's candidate for president in 1896, 1900, and 1908. In 1890, as a Democrat, Čapek was elected to the Nebraska House of Representatives from Omaha's Douglas County. Two years later, he campaigned for police judge but was defeated by the same Louis Berka who may have inspired him to become an attorney. Čapek ascribed his defeat to the influence of the Nativist American Protective Association, which attacked him as a lackey of the Pope after he addressed the congregation of a Catholic church. Čapek detested such mud-slinging, and he never again campaigned for elected office. In 1893 Čapek expressed interest in the post of U.S. consul to Prague. After Čapek's support helped him win election to the Senate, William Jennings Bryan nominated Čapek for the Prague post, but it went instead to Jan Karel (1851-1914), a Chicago banker. This was the final act in Čapek's political career.[46]

Čapek's departure from Omaha was prompted by his marriage to Anna Vostrovská, whom he met and courted during the Columbian Exposition in Chicago in August 1893. The two were married on October 20, 1894, in San José, California, where Anna lived with her parents. Evidently, Čapek did not consider his income and prospects in Omaha adequate to his new responsibilities, because instead of returning there, he and his wife first settled in Pittsburgh, then moved to New York in late January 1895. Here, later that year, their son, Thomas Jr., was born. In December 1899 Čapek opened a law office in an office building on Manhattan's East 72nd Street. He offered a full range of legal services to his clients, mostly Czechs, but concentrated on real estate, and the income from his practice satisfied him from the start. In 1908 the *Ústřední banka českých spořitelen* (Central Bank of Czech Savings Institutions) requested Čapek to prepare a report on financial conditions in New York's Czech community, and a year later, the bank's director, Jan Pátek traveled to New York to investigate the feasibility and means of establishing a Czech bank there. This bank, christened the Bank of Europe, opened in Manhattan on June 5, 1910, with Čapek as vice president. In 1912 he became president and remained so until the Bank of Europe was dissolved on August 28, 1931, as one of 2,302 American banks that failed that year.[47]

Čapek's two decades as a bank president were the height of his professional career. During this period, Čapek was the subject of an article in *Forbes*, a leading national business magazine. The article was part of a series titled "Successful Immigrants" and focused on Čapek's achievement as a "self-made man" and on his legacy as an immigrant who exemplified upward mobility and affirmed the notion of America as the "land of opportunity." Čapek the bank president was contrasted with the Čapek who arrived four decades earlier with $12 in his pocket and "longed for the opportunity to fulfill his youthful dream of knowledge and riches." Summarizing his own steps to success, Čapek advised young Czech immigrants to learn English, obtain an education, become citizens (as Čapek did in 1886), develop the drive to overcome adversity, and join American society.[48]

Čapek's other lifelong endeavor, the one that makes him even more worthy of a biographical monograph than his record as a "self-made man," was to study and write about the Czechs in America, as well as to contribute to the development of their cultural life and to the formation of their image in American society. Čapek is remembered primarily as an early and prolific author of books and pamphlets about Czech-America. He also did important work on behalf of his ethnic group in other roles, especially as journalist and community spokesman.

Not surprisingly, Čapek's first role in Czech-American affairs was as a journalist: he arrived in New York to live with his brother, who had spent most of the preceding eight years as a newspaper editor and was well known to his countrymen in America in that capacity. In Jan Vratislav Čapek's household, Thomas became acquainted with the leading Czech-American periodicals, as well as with František Škarda (1848-1900), who was a frequent guest. Škarda was also owner of *Dělnické listy*, and Thomas Čapek began his journalistic career on this newspaper. This career did not end after his resignation from the Omaha *Pokrok západu* in 1886 to pursue a university degree and a career in law: during summer vacation the following year, he lived in the Chicago home of August Geringer (1842-1930), the leading Czech publisher in America, and worked as a law reporter for Geringer's daily, *Svornost* (Concord) (October 8, 1875-1957). In 1892 in Omaha, when he was already a practicing attorney, Čapek became editor and, as a member of the Bohemian American National Committee, co-founder and co-publisher of the monthly *Bohemian Voice* (September 1892-November 1894). This was the first Czech-American periodical in the English language, and it attempted to make the Czechs better known in the United States, both as a European nation and as an American immigrant ethnic group. Articles about key Czech historical figures, such as Jan Amos Komenský, contemporary artists and politicians, for instance Antonín Dvořák, Božena Němcová, and František Ladislav Rieger, and leading Czech-Americans, e.g. Karel Jonáš, were a regular feature, as were English translations of Czech literature. For example, Čapek himself translated *"Přivedla žebráka na mizinu,"* a story from Jan Neruda's *Povídky malostránské* (Tales from Prague's Malá Strana), under the English title "How She Ruined a Beggar." Because of his impending marriage and departure from Omaha, Čapek resigned as editor of the *Bohemian Voice* in April 1894, and Josef Jiří Král edited the last eight issues. After the *Bohemian Voice*, Čapek never joined the staff of another periodical. He did however, occasionally contribute articles to the Czech-American and even mainstream American press, such as a 1901 interview with the Russian anarchist Petr Alekseevich Kropotkin for *New-Yorské listy* (New York Pages) (August 9, 1886-June 8, 1966) and a 1903 report from Bulgaria for the *New York Times*.[49]

Čapek's books and pamphlets were a natural outgrowth of his work as a journalist. In 1883 while he was Thomas Čapek's and Jan Vratislav Čapek's partner as owner and editor of *Patriot*, František Bartošek published a book titled *První Čech v Americe: dějepisná stat* (The First Czech in America: a Historical Essay). Bartošek's book may have inspired or influenced Thomas Čapek, because just two years after the book's appearance, Čapek began publishing a serialized article on the earliest Czech immigrants to America in *Květy americké* (American Blossoms) (October 15, 1884-1887). In 1889 Čapek contributed a series of articles on the same theme to *Pokrok západu*, whose editor and Čapek's former employer, Jan Rosický, also issued them, on his own initiative, as a book titled *Památky českých emigrantů v Americe: příspěvek k dějinám česko-amerického vystěhovalectví* (Traces of Czech Emigrants in America: a Contribution to the History of the Czech-American Emigration). Another book that grew out of Čapek's career in journalism was *Padesát let českého tisku v Americe* (Fifty Years of the Czech Press in America). The years of painstaking research that underlie this major historical study and bibliography were an accomplishment that could not be duplicated today. Through his experience as a journalist, Čapek had gained a thorough knowledge of the subject and developed the credibility and personal relationships that gave him access to the most desirable informants and their archives. *Padesát let českého tisku v Americe* describes many periodicals, individuals, and events that were already obscure in Čapek's day. Today Čapek's reputation and relevance in Czech-American historiography still rest largely on this book.[50]

A seventeen-year hiatus followed Rosický's publication of Čapek's first book. In 1906 Čapek published *The Slovaks of Hungary: Slavs and Panslavism*. With this second book, Čapek introduced himself as a publicist for Czech, Slovak, and Slavic interests. He wrote for an American audience that might otherwise form its opinions about the Slovaks on the basis of pro-Hungarian sources, which denied the existence of a Slovak nation or at least doubted the viability of such a nation. The polemical nature of another work, *Bohemia under Hapsburg Misrule*, which Čapek edited in the midst of World War I, was evident from its very title. The earnestness with which Čapek took up the role of publicist for his people is evident in the effect of the war years on the development of his most important published work. In October 1925 writing the preface to *Naše Amerika* (Our America), a work of encyclopedic breadth and richness, Čapek recalled that he began to research and write this book sixteen years earlier. The Czechoslovak independence movement that emerged while Čapek was in the midst of this work needed the support of the American government to achieve its goal. A key building block of such support was a campaign to make the American public better informed about the Czechs and favorably disposed toward Czech independence. Although it was published two years after the war ended and Czech independence was won, Čapek's *Čechs (Bohemians) in America* filled the need for an informative, general study of this ethnic group for a popular audience (and to this day remains the only study of its kind). "Foreseeing that a new world order would emerge from the war," wrote Čapek, "and that interest in the American Czechs would therefore rise, I suspended work on the Czech-language work for the time being and proceeded to form the material into an English-language manuscript." Also during this period, and in collaboration with his wife, Čapek compiled the first bibliography of sources in English about Bohemia and the Czechs. By contrast, *Naše Amerika* was not intended to publicize a little-known ethnic group and could count on a readership whose expectations and level of interest were much higher. Thus Čapek was under little pressure to rush the work into print and could afford to indulge in the kind of detailed treatment that made this text considerably more than twice the length of its English-language predecessor.[51]

The last major work Čapek undertook was a Czech-American biographical dictionary with the tentative title *Naši Američané* (Our Americans). He started work on this project around 1937, and reported in September 1939 that he "sent the manuscript to a Prague [publisher] several months before." The dictionary consisted of three parts: part one was devoted to the immigrant generation, part two to the second and subsequent generations, and part three to visitors from the Czech lands who published accounts of America after their return home. Part three was rejected and returned by the unnamed publisher in Prague, which was under Nazi occupation, and promptly published in Chicago under the title *Návštěvníci z Čech a Moravy v Americe v letech 1848-1939* (Visitors from Bohemia and Moravia in America in the Years 1848-1939). The fate of the remainder of the manuscript is a mystery. Lifka (1946) reported that it was still unpublished but said nothing about its whereabouts. *The Čapek Papers* at the Library of Congress in Washington contain some three hundred typescript biographies written by Čapek, as well as a large body of source material he used to prepare them. The relationship of this assortment of typescript biographies to the manuscript that Čapek sent to German-occupied Prague is unclear. While she was making arrangements for the transfer of her deceased husband's papers to the Library of Congress in 1953, Anna Čapková expressed the desire to use the typescript biographies to prepare and publish the biographical dictionary that Thomas Čapek had in mind. This suggests that the 1939 manuscript was not returned to the United States.[52]

Besides his work as a journalist, bibliographer, and historian, Čapek served his ethnic group in a variety of public roles. During his first sojourn in Omaha in 1884-1886, he was a teacher for one semester in a Czech Freethinking school. As early as 1889, when he was invited to address a pilgrimage to Augustin Herrman's grave organized by Czechs in Baltimore, Čapek was active as a public speaker. The *Národní výbor Čechů amerických* (Bohemian American National Committee), founded in Cedar Rapids, Iowa, in 1892, was the first of several Czech-American associations in which Čapek served. (The *Bohemian Voice*, edited by Čapek, was one of the few points on this committee's ambitious agenda of cultural initiatives ever to be realized.) In 1900 when a local election official in New York insisted that he register as an Austrian, Čapek launched a successful campaign in the courts and state legislature for the recognition of a Czech nationality. During the Russo-Japanese War of 1904-1905, Čapek organized the Slavic Alliance to promote Russian and Slavic interests in the United States, and he officially welcomed the Russian delegation that arrived to negotiate the Treaty of Portsmouth. During the same period, Čapek was chairman of the committee that established a Czech branch of the New York Public Library. Such activity made Čapek a recognized spokesman of the Czechs in America, and by October 1918, when President Woodrow Wilson backed independence for Austria's Slavs and *The New York Times* published an article titled "Slav Leaders Hail Note to Austria," Čapek was the "Slav leader" whose views were quoted first and at greatest length.[53]

Ironically, and to his subsequent regret, Čapek's role in the Czechoslovak independence movement was minor and mostly limited to attendance at various meetings and rallies. His responsibilities as a bank president and his reluctance to resign from his post prevented him from participating more actively in the movement he so ardently supported. Perhaps to make up for his prudence during the war, Čapek took the initiative to build a monument to the late President Wilson in Prague. Čapek first proposed the monument at a meeting of the Board of Directors of the Bank of Europe, organized a successful fund-raising campaign, and was the speaker of honor at the monument's unveiling ceremony on July 4, 1928. (Wilson's monument was dismantled by the Nazis while they ruled Prague, and the plaque that replaced it after the war was removed by the Communists.) Čapek's reputation as a Czech-American historian and leader reached his homeland early: in 1906 he was inducted into the *Česká národní rada* (Czech National Council) as a member of its committee for Czechs abroad, and he delivered reports to the council's meetings during his trips to Prague. Čapek also became a member of learned societies in the Czech lands, including the prestigious *Královská česká společnost nauk* (Royal Bohemian Society of

Science) and the *Rodopisná společnost československá* (Czecho-slovak Genealogical Society).[54]

On both sides of the Atlantic, Čapek continued to receive recognition and honors well into his later years. In 1936 the eminent American historian John Franklin Jameson tried to acquire Čapek's papers for the Library of Congress and even traveled to Čapek's New York home to woo Čapek. The Náprstek Museum in Prague also wanted the papers. Fiorello La Guardia appointed Čapek to the "Mayor's Committee for Czecho-Slovak Participation in the World's Fair" in New York in 1939. Čapek continued to take a vital interest in Czech-American affairs until the end of his life. Just days before his death on March 28, 1950, Čapek wrote a letter to the almanac *Amerikán* in which he discussed, among other things, a proposal he made as early as 1932 for the formation of a "Czechoslovak Historical Society" in America.[55]

Biographical Models

After identifying and evaluating the available sources, and after reviewing the subject's life, the biographer's next step is to choose and refine a model for his eventual manuscript. In *The Biographer's Craft*, Milton Lomask, an experienced biographer, identifies four common models: narrative, topical, essay, and the "and" biography, which has a double focus on an individual *and* on something else—usually a social group, institution, or historical period. Elsewhere in his book, however, Lomask devotes a chapter to psychobiography, and he dismisses the notion of an exhaustive enumeration of biographical models. "Not only are you free to experiment with form," Lomask writes, "but it is imperative that you do so—that before embarking on a full writing schedule you weigh with care the several likely ways in which your story can be told." The biographer must weigh his purpose and audience, as well as the body of sources and the nature of the subject's life, as he selects a model and develops a structure for the text he intends to write.[56]

In the case of Thomas Čapek, several different approaches are open. Thanks to Čapek's stature as a founder of Czech-American studies, a scholarly biography of him in the field of

American immigration history certainly requires no justification and presents one possible combination of purpose and audience. The body of sources documenting Čapek's life and activities is probably substantial and varied enough to support any of the models Lomask describes. Even a psychobiographer would find ample material in the sources described earlier. Many telling insights could be gleaned from a close study of Čapek's use of language, which he demonstrated at great length throughout his life in his many writings in two languages. Čapek's writings also present a profusion of the kind of personal anecdotes and details about personal habits and daily life that psychologists find especially valuable. For example, in *Moje Amerika* Čapek mentions that, after "fifty years of America," his wife still hears him speak Czech in his sleep. Other informants can be equally revealing: Josef C. Blecha, brother of Čapek's daughter-in-law, writes, "I *never* saw him dressed in casual clothes." (The emphasis on "never" is Blecha's.)[57]

Like the body of sources, the nature of Čapek's life also accommodates a variety of approaches. At least two different aspects of Čapek's life account for this variety: period and theme. The model which the biographer chooses, and the way he applies the model in his treatment of a particular life, depend on how he combines period and theme and on the relative emphasis he gives to each of these two aspects. When the primary emphasis is to be on period, then the narrative model is appropriate. This is the approach Čapek himself takes in *Moje Amerika*: the chapters are based on distinct periods in his life, such as "Chrášťovice, 1861-1873," "Omaha, 1884-1886," and so on. In his biography of Charles Jonas (Karel Jonáš), Chrislock also took this approach, and his chapter headings follow a similar pattern: "Bohemia (1840-1860)," "Wisconsin (Early 1890s)," and so forth.

By contrast, if the biographer prefers to focus on theme, then either the topical or the "and" biography are appropriate models. In a topical biography, the introductory chapters might describe Čapek's peasant family in Bohemia and his three brothers in America. Succeeding chapters might examine Čapek in turn as journalist, politician, lawyer and banker, historian and bibliographer, and Czech-American leader. Other chapters might analyze Thomas Čapek's vision of the "self-made man" and of the

"Bohemist" in America, as the world-renowned Czech writer Karel Čapek calls him in the foreword to *Moje Amerika*. The subject of immigration loomed so large in Čapek's life that more than one chapter could be devoted to it. One chapter might give an account of the Czech immigration in the United States as Čapek found it in New York, Nebraska, Cleveland, Chicago, and Pittsburgh, as well as in the places he visited. Another chapter might examine his thoughts on the immigrant's problem of identity and Čapek's lifelong personal struggle with it. Such a chapter might also consider Čapek's views on two related matters: Americanization, and the contrast between the immigrant generation and its American-born successors. Yet another aspect of immigration that deserves to be treated in a separate chapter is the problem of preserving immigrant history and Čapek's effort to salvage the Czech-American memory.

The range of possibilities for an "and" biography is also tantalizing. Potential titles spring readily to mind: "Thomas Čapek and the Czech Experience in America," or "Thomas Čapek and 'Our Americans.'" As a reference to Čapek's doomed 1939 manuscript biographical dictionary of Czech-Americans, "Our Americans" might symbolize his lifelong effort to preserve Czech-American identity and history. On another level, the vagueness of "Our Americans" brings to mind the *leitmotiv* of Čapek's life: the vague state to which the immigrant is perpetually consigned between "departure" from the Old Country and "arrival" in the New World, a state in which conflicting demands for his loyalty and his own diverging commitments and longings never leave him at rest and constantly disturb his focus, so that even a simple possessive pronoun like "our" cannot be counted on to have one clear meaning. Finally, "Our Americans" is a convenient license and *entrée* for indulging in collective biography. After all, Čapek was perhaps foremost a biographer himself, and he knew and described an impressive number of his contemporaries in the Czech-American world. In 1946 Bohumír Lifka, then (1934-1959) librarian of the Náprstek Museum in Prague, wrote what could serve as an eloquent epitaph for Thomas Čapek: "This is a man who saved for us and our descendants the memory of the souls of thousands of our countrymen whom destiny carried away across the ocean into the distant lands of the New World. . . ."[58]

Czech-Americans:
A Selected Bibliography of
Publications in English

Compiled by Miloslav Rechcígl, Jr.

Bibliographies

Jerabek, Esther, *Czechs and Slovaks in North America: A Bibliography*. New York: SVU, 1976. 448 p.

Rechcígl, Miloslav Jr., "A Classified Guide to Bibliographies Relating to Czech, Slovak, and Ruthenian Immigrants in America," *Kosmas* 7 (1988), pp. 189-212.

Rechcígl, Miloslav Jr., "Czechs, Slovaks and Ruthenians in the U.S.: A Selective Bibliography," *Czechoslovak and Central European Journal* 10, No. 1 (Summer 1991), pp. 83-132.

Historiography

Bicha, Karel D., "Czech-American Historiography: 1964-1987," *Czechoslovak and Central European Journal* 9, No. 1/2 (Summer / Winter 1990), pp. 144-150.

Opatrny, Josef, "Problems in the History of Czech Immigration to America in the Second Half of the Nineteenth Century,"

Nebraska History 74, No. 3 and 4 (Fall / Winter 1993), pp. 120-129.

Polišenský, Josef V., "Problems of Studying the History of Czech Mass Emigration to the Americas." In: *Emigration from Northern, Central, and Southern Europe: Theoretical and Methodological Principles of Research.* International Symposium. Krakow: Jagiellonian University, 1984, pp. 185-194.

Biographical Compendia

Droba, Daniel D., *Czech and Slovak Leaders in Metropolitan Chicago.* Chicago: The Slavonic Club of the University of Chicago, 1934. 307 p.

Mořkovský, Alois J., in *Short Biographies of Czech and Other Priests in Texas.* Hallettsville, TX: The Author, 1982. 183 p.

Rechcígl, Eva and Miloslav Rechcígl Jr., *SVU Directory. History, Organization and Biographies of Members.* Washington, DC: SVU Press, 1992. 390 p.

General Surveys

Čapek, Thomas, *The Čechs (Bohemians) in America.* Boston: Houghton Mifflin, 1920. 293 p. Reprinted New York: Arno Press, 1969.

Chada, Joseph, *The Czechs in the United States.* New York: SVU Press, 1981. 292 p.

Freeze, Karen Johnson, "Czechs," *Harvard Encyclopedia of American Ethnic Groups.* Cambridge, MA: Belknap Press of Harvard University, 1980. pp. 261-272.

Habenicht, Jan, *History of Czechs in America.* St. Paul, MN: Czechoslovak Genealogical Society International, 1996. 581 p.

Korytová-Margstadt, Stepanka, *To Reap a Bountiful Harvest: Czech Immigration Beyond the Mississippi, 1850-1900.* Iowa City, IA: Rudi Publications, 1993. 179 p.

Laska, Vera, *The Czechs in America 1633-1977: A Chronology and Fact Book*. Dobbs Ferry, NY: Oceana Publications, 1978. 152 p.

Miller, Kenneth D., *The Czecho-Slovaks in America*. New York: George H. Doran, 1922. 192 p.

Panorama: A Historical Review of Czechs and Slovaks in the United States. Cicero, IL: Czechoslovak National Council of America, 1971. 328 p.

Early History

Rechcígl, Miloslav Jr., "Augustine Herman Bohemiensis," *Journal of Czechoslovak and Central European Studies* 3, No. 1 (Summer 1984), pp. 139-148.

Rechcígl, Miloslav Jr., "In the Footprints of the First Czech Immigrants in America," *Czechoslovak and Central European Journal* 9 (1990), pp. 75-90.

Rechcígl, Miloslav Jr., "Early Jewish Immigrants in America from the Czech Historic Lands and Slovakia," *Rev. Soc. Hist. Czechoslovak Jews* 3 (1990-91), pp. 157-179.

Regional and Local Histories

Illinois—Reichman, John J., *Czechoslovaks of Chicago*. Chicago: Czechoslovak Historical Society of Chicago, 1937. 112 p.

Iowa—Griffith, Martha E., *The History of Czechs in Cedar Rapids. Vol. 1. 1852-1942*. Reprinted from *Iowa J. History and Politics*, vol. 42 (1944). Cedar Rapids: Czech Heritage Foundation, 1972. 96 p.; *Vol. II 1942-1982*. 1982. 111 p.

Iowa—Klimesh, Cyril A., *They Came to This Place. A History of Spillville, Iowa and its Czech Settlers*. Sebastopol, CA: Methodius Press, 1983. 239 p.

Kansas—Swehla, Francis J., "The Bohemians in Central Kansas," *Kansas State Historical Society Collections* 13 (1913-1914), pp. 469-512.

Minnesota—*New Prague, Minnesota. Brief Sketches of the History, Resources Advantages and Business Men*. New Prague, MN: The New Prague Times, 1895. 72 p.

124 • *CZECH-AMERICANS IN TRANSITION*

Minnesota—Chrislock, C. Winston, " The Czechs," in *They Chose Minnesota: A Survey of the State's Ethnic Groups*. ed. June Drenning Holmquist. St Paul: Minnesota Historical Society Press, 1981. pp. 331-351.

Minnesota—Rippley, La Vern J. and Robert J. Paulson. *German-Bohemians. The Quiet Immigrants*. Northfield, MN: St. Olaf College Press, 1995. 279 p.

Missouri—*History of the Czechs in Missouri 1845 to 1904*. St. Louis: St. Louis Genealogical Society, 1988. 71 p.

Nebraska—Rosicky, Rose, *A History of Czechs (Bohemians) in Nebraska*. Omaha: Czech Historical Society of Nebraska, 1929. 492 p. Reprinted by Whipporwill Publications (1987).

Nebraska—"The Czech-American Experience," *Nebraska History* 74, No. 3&4 (Fall/Winter 1993), pp. 101-203.

New York—Čapek, Thomas, *The Czech (Bohemian) Community of New York*. New York: America's Making, 1921. 93 p.

New York—*A History of Bohemia, Long Island*. Sayville, Long Island, NY: Weeks & Reichel Printing, 1955. 80 p.

North Dakota—Schmirler, A. A. A., *Wagon Migration. Veseleyville, D.T. 1880-1881*.Grafton, ND: Associated Printers, 1981. 242 p.

North Dakota—*Pisek. The First Century: A History of Pisek, ND and Its People*. Grafton, ND: Associated Printers, 1982. 326 p.

Ohio—Ledbetter, Eleanor E., *The Czechs of Cleveland*. Cleveland: Mayor's Advisory War Committee, 1919. 40 p.

Oklahoma—Bicha, Karel D., *The Czechs in Oklahoma*. Norman: University of Oklahoma Press, 1980. 81 p.

South Dakota—Dvorak, Joseph A., *Memorial Book History of the Czechs in the State of South Dakota*. Tabor, SD: The Czech Heritage Preservation Society, 1980. 189 p.

Texas—Maresh, H. B. and Estelle Hudson, *Czech Pioneers of the Southwest*. Dallas: South-West Press, 1934. 418 p. Reprinted Houston, TX: Western Lithograph, 1996.

Texas—*The Czechs in Texas. Papers from The Czechs in Texas: A Symposium*. Edited by Clinton Machann. College Station, TX: Texas A&M University Press, 1979. 184 p.

Texas—Machann, Clinton and James W. Mendl, *Krásná Amerika: A Study of the Texas Czechs 1851-1939*. Austin: Eakin Press, 1983. 280 p.

Texas — *Czech Voices: Stories from Texas in the Amerikán Národní Kalendář.* Translated and edited by Clinton Machann and James W. Mendl, Jr. College Station, TX: Texas A&M University Press, 1991. 147 p.

Texas — *Texas. The Remote and Near Country.* Trojanovice, Czech Republic: Obec Trojanovice, 1997. 80 p.

Texas — Strnadel, Drahomír, *Emigration to Texas from the Mistek District between 1856 and 1900.* Victoria, TX: The Czech Heritage Society of Texas, 1996. 208 p.

Texas — Gallup, Sean N., *Journeys into Czech-Moravian Texas.* College Station, TX: Texas A&M University Press, 1998. 148 p. 109 color photos.

Wisconsin — Bicha, Karel D., "The Czechs in Wisconsin History," *Wisconsin Magazine of History* 55, no. 3 (1972), pp. 194-203.

Religion

Barton, Josef J., "Religion and Cultural Change in Czech Immigrant Communities, 1850-1920." In: *Immigrants and Religion in Urban America.* eds. Randall M. Miller and Thomas D. Marzik. Philadelphia: Temple University Press, 1977, pp. 3-24.

Bicha, Karel D., "Settling Accounts with an Old Adversary: The Decatholization of Czech Immigrants in America," *Social History/Histoire Sociale* 4 (November 1972), pp. 45-60.

Čada, Joseph, *Czech-American Catholics 1850-1920.* Lisle, IL: Benedictine Abbey Press, 1964. 124 p.

Christian Sisters Union, *Unity of the Brethren in Texas 1855-1966.* Taylor, TX: Unity of the Brethren, 1970. 178 p.

Garver, Bruce M., "Czech-American Free Thinkers on the Great Plains, 1871-1914." In: *Ethnicity on the Great Plains.* ed. Frederick Luebke. Lincoln: University of Nebraska Press, 1980, pp. 147-59.

Garver, Bruce M., "Czech-American Protestants: A Minority Within a Minority," *Nebraska History* 74, No. 3&4 (Fall/Winter 1993), pp.150-167.

A History of the Czech-Moravian Catholic Communities of Texas. Translated and edited by Rev. V. A. Svrcek. Waco, TX: Texian Press, 1974. 220 p.; second printing 1983.

Kisch, Guido, *In Search of Freedom: A History of American Jews from Czechoslovakia 1740-1948.* London: E. Goldstone, 1949. 373 p.

Rechcígl, Miloslav Jr., "The Renewal and the Formation of the Moravian Church in America," *Czechoslovak and Central European Journal* 9 (1990), pp. 12-26.

Vojta, Václav, *Czechoslovak Baptists.* Minneapolis: Czechoslovak Baptist Convention in America and Canada, 1941. 276 p.

Society

Hannan, Kevin, "Ethnic Identity among the Czechs and Moravians of Texas," *Journal of American Ethnic History* 15 (Summer 1996), pp. 3-31.

Kutak, Robert ¹, *The Story of a Bohemian-American Village.* Louisville, KY: Standard Printing Co., 1933. Reprinted New York: Arno Press, 1970. 156 p.

Lynch, Russell Ward, *Czech Farmers in Oklahoma.* Stillwater: Oklahoma Agricultural and Mechanical College Press, 1942. 119 p.

Roucek, Joseph S., "Problems of Assimilation: A Study of Czechoslovaks in the United States," *Sociology and Social Research* 17 (September/ October 1931), pp. 62-71.

Roucek, Joseph S., "The American Czechs, Slovaks and Slavs in the Development of America's Climate of Opinion." In: *Czechoslovakia Past and Present.* Vol. 1. ed. Miloslav Rechcígl Jr. The Hague: Mouton, 1968, pp. 815-843.

Skrabanek, R. L., "Forms of Cooperation and Mutual Aid in a Czech-American Rural Community," *Southwestern Social Science Quarterly* 30, No. 3 (December 1949), pp. 83-88.

Skrabanek, R. L., "Social Life in a Czech-American Rural Community," *Rural Sociology* 15, No. 3 (September 1950), pp. 221-231.

Skrabanek, R. L., "The Influence of Cultural Backgrounds on Farming Practices in a Czech-American Rural Community." *Southwestern Social Science Quarterly* 31, No. 4 (March 1951), pp. 258-267.

Skrabanek, Robert L., *We're Czechs*. College Station, TX: Texas A&M University Press, 1988. 240 p.

Public Life

Chrislock, C. Winston, *Charles Jonas 1840-1896: Czech National Liberal, Wisconsin Bourbon Democrat*. Philadelphia: Balch IES Press, 1993. 216 p.

Gottfried, Alex, *Boss Cermak of Chicago: A Study of Political Leadership*. Seattle, WA: University of Washington Press, 1962. 459 p.

Laska, Vera, "Czechs and Slovaks." In: *America's Ethnic Politics*. eds. Joseph S. Roucek and Bernard Eisenberg. Westport: Greenwood Press, 1982, pp. 133-53.

Rechcígl, Miloslav Jr., *U.S. Legislators with Czechoslovak Roots from Colonial Times to Present: With Genealogical Lineages*. Washington, DC: SVU Press, 1987. 65 p.

Cultural Life

Bodnar, John, "Schooling and the Slavic American Family." In: *American Education and the European Immigrant: 1840-1940*. Urbana: University of Illinois Press, 1982, p. ?

Czechoslovak-American Puppetry. Edited by Vit Horejs. New York: GOH Productions / Seven Loaves, 1994. 80 p.

Duben, Vojtech N., "Czech and Slovak Press Outside Czechoslovakia." In *The Czechoslovak Contribution to World Culture*. ed. Miloslav Rechcígl Jr. Hague: Mouton, 1964 pp. 528-545.

Dvornik, Francis, *Czech Contributions to the Growth of the United States*. Chicago: Benedictine Abbey Press, 1962. 109 p.

Lowenbach, Jan, "Czech Composers and Musicians in America," *Musical Quarterly* 29 (1943), pp. 313-328.

Murphy, David, "Dramatic Expressions: Czech Theatre Curtains in Nebraska," *Nebraska History* 74, No. 3 and 4 (Fall / Winter 1993), pp. 168-182.

Nolte, Claire E., "Our Brothers Across the Ocean: The Czech Sokol in America to 1914," *Czechoslovak and Central European Journal* 11, No. 2 (Winter 1993), pp. 15-37.

Papers from Czech Music in Texas: A Sesquicentennial Symposium. Edited by Clinton Machann. College Station, TX: Komensky Press, 1988. 182 p.

Rechcígl, Miloslav Jr., "Czech Contributions to American Scientific and Technological Thought," *Kosmas. Czechoslovak and Central European Journal* 12, No. 1 (Summer 1996), pp. 81-99.

Rechcígl, Miloslav Jr., *Educators with Czechoslovak Roots: U.S. and Canadian Faculty Roster.* Washington: SVU Press, 1980. 122 p.

Rechcígl, Miloslav Jr. and Jiri Nehnevajsa, "American Scholars and Scientists with Czechoslovak Roots—Some Key Characteristics," *Journal of Washington Academy of Science* 58 (1968), pp. 213-222.

Rechcígl, Miloslav Jr., "Moravian Footprints in America," *Ročenka. Yearbook of the Czechoslovak Genealogical Society International* 3 (1997-1998), pp. 35-43.

Šolle, Zdenčk, "Vojtech Naprstek and His Era: Bohemia, the United States, and the Transmission of Cultures," *East Central Europe* 17, No. 1 (Spring 1990), pp. 1-30.

Sturm, Rudolf, "Czech Literature in America," in *Ethnic Literature since 1776. The Many Voices of America.* Lubbock: Texas Technical University, 1978, pp. 161-173.

Zizka, Ernest J., *Czech Cultural Contributions.* Chicago: Benedictine Abbey Press, 1942. 145 p.

Notes

1. See his *Geschichte und Zustande der Deutschen in Amerika*. Cincinnati, OH: Eggers and Wulkop, 1847.

2. *Ottův Slovník Naučný*. Praha: J. Otto, 1890, vol. 3, pp. 618-619.

3. For more information about Bakalář and his work, see Jiří Hrubeš's article in *Ibero-Americana Pragensis*, vol. 9 (1975), pp. 167-179.

4. Cited by Josef Polišenský, in *Český Lid*, vol. 88, No. 1 (1981), p. 5.

5. See Josef Polišenský et al., *Dějiny Latinské Ameriky*. Praha: Svoboda, 1979.

6. For more information, see David B. Quinn, *Set Fair for Roanoke: Voyages and Colonies, 1584-1606*. Chapel Hill: University of North Carolina Press, 1985.

7. For a recent appraisal of Augustine Herman's life and his achievements, see my study, "Augustine Herman Bohemiensis," *Kosmas*, vol. 3 (Summer 1984), pp. 139-148.

8. See Thomas Čapek, *Ancestry of Frederick Philipse, First Lord and Founder of Philipse Manor at Yonkers, NY.* New York: Paebar Co., 1939.

9. Some information about the early Czech settlers in American can be found in Thomas Čapek's book, *The Čechs (Bohemians) in America*. Boston: Houghton Mifflin Co., 1920, pp. 1,418.

10. Information on the Czech Jesuits in Latin America is based on my, heretofore unpublished, study. Some information can also be found in Vlastimil Kybal's article," Czechs and Slovaks in Latin America." In: *The Czechoslovak Contribution to World Culture*. Edited by Miloslav Rechcígl, Jr. The Hague: Mouton, 1964, pp. 516-522.

11. For more information on Moravian Brethren and their work in America, see my two earlier articles, "The Renewal and the Formation of the

Moravian Church in America," *Czechoslovak and Central European Journal*, vol. 9 (1990), pp. 12-26; "Moravian Brethren from Bohemia, Moravia and Silesia: Their Arrival and Settlement in America," *Bohemia*, vol. 32, No. 1 (1991), pp. 152-65.

12. Augustine Herman Bohemiensis, op.cit. (Endnote 7).

13. Georgetown University Library, Special Collections, Richard Crane Papers, Box 5, Folder 20, Prague, July 21, 1919.

14. Georgetown University Library, Special Collections, Richard Crane Papers, Box 5, Folder 23, Prague, August 14, 1919.

15. Ibid.

16. NARA, Decimal File 1910-29, 860F.OOB/2, Box 9381, Prague, December 7, 1920, and 860F .00/142, Box 9379, Prague, December 11, 1920.

17. NARA, Decimal File 1910-29, 860F.00/67, Box 9379.

18. About the Crane-Masaryk relationship see the introduction to: Crane, John O., and Sylvia Crane: *Czechoslovakia: Anvil of the Cold War*. Praeger, 1982; Kovtun, George: *Masaryk and America: Testimony of a Relationship*. Washington, D.C., Library of Congress, 1988. I used also the manuscript of the article "Charles R. Crane: Godfather to Czechoslovakia," which the author Betty Miller Unterberger kindly gave me before the article was published.

19. Einstein, Lewis: *A Diplomat Looks Back*. Yale University Press, 1968.

20. Kennan, George F.: *Memoirs*. Boston, 1967 (Vol. I), 1972 (Vol. II).; *From Prague after Munich: Diplomatic Papers 1939-1940*. Princeton University Press, 1959.

21. Einstein refers to Masaryk's defense (1899) of Leopold Hilsner, a Jew accused of ritual murder in a prominent trial, and to Masaryk's lead (1886) in exposing the Královédvorský and Zelenohorský Manuscripts, forgeries attributed to Václav Hanka (1791-1861) which quickly became icons of Czech nationalism after their discovery in 1817-1818. See also Derek Sayer, *The Coasts of Bohemia: a Czech History* (Princeton University Press, 1998), 144-145, and Podiven, *Češi v dějinách nové doby* (Praha: Rozmluvy, 1991), 185-188. ("Podiven" is the collective pseudonym of Petr Příhoda, Milan Otáhal, and Petr Pithart.)

22. Einstein, op.cit., pp.193-198.

23. NARA, Decimal File 1910-29, 860F.002128, Box 9381, Prague, January 10, 1923.

24. NARA, Decimal File 1910-29, 860F.00/59, Box 6615, Prague, July 25, 1935.

25. NARA, Decimal File 1910-29, 860F.00/51, Box 6615, Prague, September 4, 1935.

26. NARA, Decimal File 1910-29, 860F.002/77, Box 6615, Prague, October 31, 1935.

27. NARA, Decimal File 1910-29, 860F.00/406, Box 6613, Prague, January 7, 1936.

28. About the diplomatic career of Wilbur Carr see Crane, Katharine: *Mr. Carr of State. Forty-Seven Years in the Department of State*. St. Martin's Press, New York 1960. The last two chapters of this book, "Minister to Czechoslovakia" and "Coming of Hitler," describe Carr as the U.S. Minister in Prague.

29. Clinton Machann and James W. Mendl, Jr., transl. and ed., *Czech*

voices: Stories from Texas in the Amerikán Národní Kalendár, 1st ed. (College Station, TX: Texas A&M University Press, 1991). C. Winston Chrislock, *Charles Jonas (1840-1896): Czech National Liberal, Wisconsin Bourbon Democrat* (Philadelphia: Balch Institute Press; London and Cranbury, NJ: Associated University Presses, 1993). Zdeněk Šolle, *Vojta Náprstek a jeho doba* (Praha: Felis, 1994).

30. Thomas Čapek, *The Čechs (Bohemians) in America: a Study of Their National, Cultural, Political, Social, Economic and Religious Life* (Boston, New York: Houghton Mifflin Company, 1920; reprint, New York: Arno Press, 1969; reprint, Westport, Conn., Greenwood Press 1970). Thomas Čapek, *Naše Amerika* (V Praze: Nakl. Národní rady Československé, 1926). Thomas Čapek and Anna Vostrovský Čapek, *Bohemian (Čech) Bibliography: a Finding List of Writings in English Relating to Bohemia and the Čechs* (New York: Fleming H. Revell company, 1918). Thomas Čapek, *The Slovaks of Hungary: Slavs and Panslavism* (New York: Knickerbocker Press, 1906). Thomas Čapek, ed., *Bohemia under Hapsburg Misrule: a Study of the Ideals and Aspirations of the Bohemian and Slovak Peoples, as They Relate to and are Affected by the Great European War* (New York, Chicago, etc.: Fleming H. Revell company, 1915).

31. Čeněk Zíbrt, "Američtí Čechové ve světle nových spisů J. Salaby, T. Čapka a J. Habenichta," *Časopis Musea Království Českého* 85 (1911): 330-387. Augustín Seifer, "Vzácný český krajan Tomáš Čapek v New Yorku," *Naše zahraničí* 7 (1926): 206-208. Bohumir Lifka, *Historiograf české Ameriky Tomáš Čapek* (Praha: Rodopisná společnost československá, 1947). Jaroslav E. S. Vojan, "Tomáš Čapek, historik české Ameriky," *Amerikán národní kalendář* 56 (1933): 199-202.

32. Thomas Čapek, *Moje Amerika, vzpomínky a úvahy, 1861-1934* (Praha: F. Borový, 1935). Hereinafter cited as *MA*.

33. Thomas Čapek, *Jan Vratislav Čapek, Českoamerický buditel, žurnalista a vynálezce* (Praha: Rolnická tiskárna, 1921). Thomas Čapek, *Z New Yorku do Prahy a zpět: vyňatky z listů (psaných původně anglicky), jež spisovatel zasílal své ženě z cesty New York-Cherbourg-Paříž-Praha-Berlín-Londýn-Liverpool-New York, v říjnu, listopadu a prosinci 1921* (V Praze: Kočí, 1922).

34. *MA*, 75-77, 95, 211.

35. The numerous references in *MA* to Rosický, Roosevelt, Vanderbilt, Bryan, and Masaryk can be found in the index.

36. "Chráštovice, 1861-1873," in *MA*, 9-36.

37. *MA*, 27, 79. Venuše Kocková, electronic mail messages to author, March 23 and April 2, 1998.

38. Ludmila Leong to author, March 1998.

39. *MA*, 20-21. Čapek, *Jan Vratislav Čapek*, 6, 10.

40. "Písek, 1873-1876," in *MA*, 37-41. "Strakonice, 1876-1879," in *MA*, 42-43.

41. *MA*, 32, 45-46.

42. Čapek, *Jan Vratislav Čapek*, 6-8, 10. Thomas Čapek, *Padesát let českého tisku v Americe od vydání "Slowana amerikánského" v Racine, dne I. ledna 1860 do I. ledna 1910, s doplňky do začátku 1911* (New York: Bank of

Europe, 1911), 111, 113-114, 121-122. *MA*, 44. The dates of arrival of Jan Vratislav Čapek and Ladislav Matěj Čapek are from Leo Bača, electronic mail message to author, March 30, 1998. Bača is the author of *Czech Immigration Passenger Lists* (Halletsville, TX.: Old Homestead Pub. Co., 1983).

43. Just on pp. 76, 96, 98, and 147 in *MA*, Čapek uses the term "self-made man" to describe six individuals, and he discusses the term itself on pp. 125-126.

44. *MA*, 46-54, 58-60. Čapek, *Jan Vratislav Čapek*, 12.

45. *MA*, 54-58, 67, 71, 75.

46. Vojan, "Čapek," 200. *MA*, 69, 94-95, 97-100. Chrislock, *Charles Jonas*.

47. *MA*, 102-107, 110, 155-156, 241-246.

48. Genevieve Parkhurst, "Czech Who Becomes Bank President," *Forbes Magazine* 3 (1919): 698.

49. *MA*, 100-102, 166, 187. A facsimile reproduction of the cover of *The Bohemian Voice*, v. 1, no. 1 (September 1, 1892) appears in Čapek, *Bohemian Bibliography*, 220. For citations to key articles published in *The Bohemian Voice*, see Čapek, *Bohemian Bibliography*, 67, 81-82, 106, 144-146. Thomas Čapek, "Interview s učencem-revolucionářem," *New-Yorské listy*, April 7, 1901. Thomas Čapek, "Complications of the Balkan Problem," *New York Times*, October 26, 1903.

50. František Bartošek, *První Čech v Americe: dějepisná stat*, Sbírka zábavného čtení, sv. 1. (New York: *Dělník americký*, 1883). Tomáš Čapek, "První Čechové američtí" (First American Czechs), *Květy americké* 2 (1885-1886): 29-30, 45-46 and 3 (1886-87): 11-12, 28-29, 44-46, 60-61, 76-77. "K dějinám prvních amerických Čechů" (On the History of the First American Czechs), *Květy americké* 2 (1885-1886): 376. *MA*, 235. Thomas Čapek, *Památky českých emigrantů v Americe: příspěvek k dějinám česko-amerického vystěhovalectví* (Omaha: *Pokrok západu*, 1889; 2nd, corrected ed., Omaha: Národní tiskárny, 1907).

51. Čapek, *Naše Amerika*, 8.

52. Tomáš Čapek, foreword to *Návštěvníci z Čech a Moravy v Americe v letech 1848-1939, příspěvek k dějinám amerických Čechů* (Chicago: Color Printing Co., 1940). Lifka, *Historiograf*, 10-11. Alan L. Heyneman to Lewis C. Coffin, June 15, 1953, case file, Čapek Papers, Manuscript Division, Library of Congress.

53. *MA*, 86, 89, 100-101, 161-164, 167, 196-201. "Slav Leaders Hail Note to Austria," *New York Times*, October 20, 1918.

54. *MA*, 209-211, 222-226, 229. For a portrait of Čapek with Czechoslovak President Masaryk and others at the Wilson monument unveiling ceremony, see plate after p. 236 in *MA*. Zdeněk Hojda and Jiří Pokorný, *Pomníky a zapomníky* (Monuments and Non-monuments) (Praha and Litomyšl: Paseka, 1996), 183-186, 190, 256. Seifert, "Vzácný český krajan," 206. Vojan, "Tomáš Čapek," 202. Lifka, "Historiograf," 3.

55. John Franklin Jameson to Thomas A. Čapek, September 28, 1936, in *An Historian's World: Selections from the Correspondence of John Franklin Jameson*, ed. Elizabeth Donnan and Leo F. Stock. (Philadelphia: American Philosophical Society, 1956), 362-363. Read Lewis to Jameson, October 30,

1936, case file, Čapek Papers, Manuscript Division, Library of Congress. Čapek to Jameson, November 5 & 11, 1936, case file, Čapek Papers, Manuscript Division, Library of Congress. Fiorello La Guardia to Čapek, July 25, 1939, Box 14, folder 1, Čapek Papers, Manuscript Division, Library of Congress. Tomáš Čapek, "Jsme Američané či ne?" (Are We Americans or Not?), *Amerikán: národní kalendář* 74 (1951), 19-20.

56. Milton Lomask, *The Biographer's Craft* (New York: Harper & Row, 1986), 2-4. Lomask, "Psychobiography," in *The Biographer's Craft*, 121-131.

57. *MA*, 155. Joseph C. Blecha to author, March 23, 1998.

58. Lifka, "Historiograf," 3.

About the Authors

LEO BACA has published historical and genealogical works related to Czech Americans, including *Czech Immigration Passenger Lists*, and has lectured widely on the subject of Czech immigration to Texas.

PETER M. BÍSEK is the publisher and editor of the Czech-American independent bi-weekly *Americké Listy* (formerly *Československý Týdeník*).

DAVID Z. CHROUST, who specializes in ethnic libraries and Germanic and Slavic collections, is a librarian at Texas A&M University, where he is currently building a Czech collection.

LUDMILA DUTKOVÁ, a native of the Haná region of Moravia, is a Ph.D. candidate in the Interdisciplinary Program in Second Language Acquisition and Teaching at the University of Arizona in Tucson.

DANIEL HRNA, a Houston attorney and member of the Board of Trustees of the Czech Heritage Society of Texas, is compiling information about the contributions of Czech-Americans to the social and political life of Texas.

ROBERT JANAK, a public school teacher from Beaumont, is a member of the Board of Trustees of the Czech Heritage Society of Texas and the author of several publications on the Czech heritage of Texas.

135

ZDENĚK LYČKA, an engineer, philologist, and translator, has long been associated with the Czech Ministry of Foreign Affairs, where he recently served as director of cultural relations and Czechs living abroad.

CLINTON MACHANN, professor of English at Texas A&M University, is chairman of the Board of Directors of the Czech Educational Foundation of Texas and the author of several books and articles about Texas Czechs.

LEONARD MIKESKA is vice-president of the Slavonic Benevolent Order of the State of Texas (SPJST).

MILADA POLIŠENKÁ, a Czech historian and recently a visiting professor of history at Texas Tech University, has completed a book manuscript on Czechoslovak citizens deported to Soviet labor camps (1945-1950) and has co-edited a collection of documents on early Czechoslovak foreign policy.

MILOSLAV RECHCÍGL, JR., a retired scientist, former research director for the U.S. Agency for International Development, and author of numerous publications on early Czech immigration to America, was one of the founders and serves as the current president of the Czechoslovak Society of Arts and Sciences.

JOSEPH N. ROŠTINSKÝ, professor of European civilization studies at the University of Tokai in Tokyo, has published various articles on Czech, German, and Russian semiotics, and he recently helped to establish the department of Japanese at Masaryk University in Brno.

ALEXANDR VONDRA, a Czech diplomat, journalist, and geographer who was one of the signatories of Charter 77, a co-founder of the Civic Forum, and an advisor to President Václav Havel, is the Ambassador of the Czech Republic to the United States.